The Up & Running Series from SYBEX

Other titles include Up & Running with:

- AutoSketch 3
- Carbon Copy Plus
- Clipper 5.01
- DOS 3.3
- DOS 5
- DR DOS 5.0
- Flight Simulator
- Grammatik IV 2.0
- Harvard Graphics
- Lotus 1-2-3 Release 2.2
- Lotus 1-2-3 Release 2.3
- Lotus 1-2-3 Release 3.1
- Norton Utilities
- Norton Utilities 5
- Norton Utilities on the Macintosh
- PageMaker 4 on the PC
- PageMaker on the Macintosh
- PC Tools Deluxe 6
- PC-Write
- Q&A
- Q&A 4
- Quattro Pro 3
- Quicken 4
- ToolBook for Windows
- Turbo Pascal 5.5
- Windows 3.0
- Windows 286/386
- Word for Windows
- WordPerfect 5.1
- WordPerfect Library/Office PC
- XTreeGold 2
- Your Hard Disk

Computer users are not all alike. Neither are SYBEX books.

We know our customers have a variety of needs. They've told us so. And because we've listened, we've developed several distinct types of books to meet the needs of each of our customers. What are you looking for in computer help?

If you're looking for the basics, try the **ABC's** series, or for a more visual approach, select **Teach Yourself**.

Mastering and **Understanding** titles offer you a step-by-step introduction, plus an in-depth examination of intermediate-level features, to use as you progress.

Our **Up & Running** series is designed for computer-literate consumers who want a no-nonsense overview of new programs. Just 20 basic lessons, and you're on your way.

SYBEX **Encyclopedias** provide a comprehensive reference and explanation of all of the commands, features and functions of the subject software.

Sometimes a subject requires a special treatment that our standard series doesn't provide. So you'll find we have titles like **Advanced Techniques, Handbooks, Tips & Tricks**, and others that are specifically tailored to satisfy a unique need.

You'll find SYBEX publishes a variety of books on every popular software package. Looking for computer help? Help Yourself to SYBEX.

For a complete catalog of our publications:

SYBEX Inc.
2021 Challenger Drive, Alameda, CA 94501
Tel: (415) 523-8233/(800) 227-2346 Telex: 336311
Fax: (415) 523-2373

Up & Running with PROCOMM® PLUS 2.0
Second Edition

■ ■ ■ ■ ■ ■ ■ ■ ■ ■ ■

Bob Campbell

San Francisco ■ Paris ■ Düsseldorf ■ Soest

Acquisitions Editor: Dianne King
Series Editor: Joanne Cuthbertson
Editor: Stefan Grünwedel
Technical Editor: Jon Forrest
Word Processors: Ann Dunn and Susan Trybull
Book Designers: Ingrid Owen and Helen Bruno
Icon Designer: Helen Bruno
Screen Graphics: Cuong Le
Desktop Production Artists: Claudia Smelser and Lucie Živny
Proofreader: Catherine Mahoney
Indexer: Ted Laux
Cover Designer: Archer Design
Screen reproductions produced by XenoFont.

PROCOMM PLUS is a trademark of Datastorm Technologies, Inc.
XenoFont is a trademark of XenoSoft.

SYBEX is a registered trademark of SYBEX. Inc.

TRADEMARKS: SYBEX has attempted throughout this book to distinguish proprietary trademarks from descriptive terms by following the capitalization style used by the manufacturer.

SYBEX is not affiliated with any manufacturer.

Every effort has been made to supply complete and accurate information. However, SYBEX assumes no responsibility for its use, nor for any infringement of the intellectual property rights of third parties which would result from such use.

First Edition copyright ©1991 SYBEX Inc.
Copyright ©1991 SYBEX Inc., 2021 Challenger Drive, Alameda, CA 94501.
World rights reserved. No part of this publication may be stored in a retrieval system, transmitted, or reproduced in any way, including but not limited to photocopy, photograph, magnetic or other record, without the prior agreement and written permission of the publisher.

Library of Congress Card Number: 91-65969
ISBN: 0-89588-879-3

Manufactured in the United States of America
10 9 8 7 6

SYBEX Up & Running Books

■ ■ ■ ■ ■ ■ ■ ■ ■ ■

The Up & Running series of books from SYBEX has been developed for committed, eager PC users who would like to become familiar with a wide variety of programs and operations as quickly as possible. We assume that you are comfortable with your PC and that you know the basic functions of word processing, spreadsheets, and database management. With this background, Up & Running books will show you in 20 steps what particular products can do and how to use them.

Who this book is for

Up & Running books are designed to save you time and money. First, you can avoid purchase mistakes by previewing products before you buy them—exploring their features, strengths, and limitations. Second, once you decide to purchase a product, you can learn its basics quickly by following the 20 steps—even if you are a beginner.

What this book provides

The first step usually covers software installation in relation to hardware requirements. You'll learn whether the program can operate with your available hardware as well as various methods for starting the program. The second step often introduces the program's user interface. The remaining 18 steps demonstrate the program's basic functions, using examples and short descriptions.

Contents & structure

A clock shows the amount of time you can expect to spend at your computer for each step. Naturally, you'll need much less time if you only read through the step rather than complete it at your computer.

Special symbols and notes

You can also focus on particular points by scanning the short notes in the margins and locating the sections you are most interested in.

vii

In addition, three symbols highlight particular sections of text:

The Action symbol highlights important steps that you will carry out.

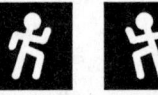

The Tip symbol indicates a practical hint or special technique.

The Warning symbol alerts you to a potential problem and suggestions for avoiding it.

We have structured the Up & Running books so that the busy user spends little time studying documentation and is not burdened with unnecessary text. An Up & Running book cannot, of course, replace a lengthier book that contains advanced applications. However, you will get the information you need to put the program to practical use and to learn its basic functions in the shortest possible time.

We welcome your comments

SYBEX is very interested in your reactions to the Up & Running series. Your opinions and suggestions will help all of our readers, including yourself. Please send your comments to: SYBEX Editorial Department, 2021 Challenger Drive, Alameda, CA 94501.

Preface

■ ■ ■ ■ ■ ■ ■ ■ ■

This book is an introduction to PROCOMM PLUS, whose ease of use and reasonable price have made it one of the most popular communications programs in the world. By working through the examples, you will learn how to call an online service and find the information you want, how to send and receive files, how to automate complex and hard-to-remember procedures, how to operate and contact your own bulletin board, and much more.

If you have used earlier versions of PROCOMM PLUS, you will find Version 2.0 (or 2.01), covered in this book, well worth an upgrade. It offers a much more powerful script language for automating your operations, a more capable editor, and better file-transfer protocols and terminal emulation, among other improvements.

Many of the examples in this book make use of CompuServe, a popular and inexpensive online service available via local telephone numbers around most of the country. In fact, you probably received a free introductory CompuServe membership with your copy of PROCOMM PLUS, and so you should be able to replicate the examples with your own CompuServe account. Where necessary, the book introduces another online system to illustrate a function not applicable to CompuServe.

PROCOMM PLUS makes only modest hardware requirements on your system. To use it, you need an IBM PC or compatible with at least 192K of free memory, at least one floppy disk drive (and preferably a hard disk), and a modem connected to an ordinary telephone line. If you have an external modem, it must be connected to a serial port on your computer through a proper cable. The examples assume that you have a Hayes-compatible modem; otherwise, you may have to adapt them to your own system.

These items provided, you can proceed with confidence to set up and use PROCOMM PLUS and to appreciate how its intuitive approach to communications will open varied worlds online to you.

To pursue PROCOMM PLUS and serial communications in greater depth, please see my book, *Understanding PROCOMM PLUS 2.0* (SYBEX, 1991).

Bob Campbell, July 1991

Table of Contents

Step 1
Installation 1

Step 2
Working with
PROCOMM PLUS 7

Step 3
Checking
Your Setup 17

Step 4
Using the Dialing
Directory 21

Step 5
Dialing
Remote Systems 31

Step 6
Going
Online 37

Step 7
Receiving
a File 43

Step 8
Sending
a File 49

Step 9
Using the
Editor 53

Step 10
Making ASCII
File Transfers 59

Step 11
Using
External Protocols 65

Step 12
Using
Kermit 71

Step 13
Record
Keeping 77

Step 14
Using
Meta Keys 83

Step 15
Using
Scripts 87

Step 16
Writing Your
Own Scripts 93

Step 17
Your Own
Bulletin Board 101

Step 18
Using
External Programs 111

Step 19
Using
Terminal Emulations 117

Step 20
Customizing
Your System 125

Installation

To install PROCOMM PLUS, you need only make backup copies of your distribution disks, run the setup program provided, and make a couple of small modifications to your setup.

BACKING UP YOUR PROGRAM DISKS

As when installing any new software, make backup copies of your distribution disks before you do anything else and put the originals away for safekeeping. Use the DOS DISKCOPY command to copy each of the two or three disks in the format that you will use (3½-inch or 5¼-inch). Label each copy and use the copies for the actual installation described in the next section.

If you are installing the program to run from a floppy-disk drive, you will need an additional formatted disk as a working disk. Use a disk of the highest capacity that will work in your drive. If you *must* use a 360K floppy, it should not be a bootable disk—otherwise there will not be enough room for all the PROCOMM PLUS files that you need.

Floppy-disk systems

STEP 1

Beginning the installation

RUNNING THE INSTALLATION PROGRAM

Load your copy of the program disk into drive A of your computer. If you are using a two floppy-drive system, load your working disk into drive B. Enter the command

    a:pcinstal

Follow these steps to install the program on your system:

1. At the opening screen, if you are asked, type **y** (or press Enter) if the copyright box appears in blue, or type **n** if it doesn't. If you have a color video adapter, PCINSTAL asks this question in case you have a black-and-white monitor. If you do, it will install PROCOMM PLUS to run in black-and-white.

2. After you have read the opening message and pressed any key, type **i** and press Enter to install PROCOMM PLUS for the first time, or type **u** and press Enter to upgrade your system from an earlier version of PROCOMM PLUS.

3. Enter the path from which PCINSTAL is running, or just press Enter if the path shown is correct.

4. If you have a hard disk, PCINSTAL will ask whether you want to install the program on it. Press **y** if you do. If you are installing on a floppy drive, highlight the correct statement from the menu and press Enter—for instance, if you indicate that your disk in drive B has a higher capacity than the one in drive A, PCINSTAL will install the program on the disk in drive B. Insert your working disk into the target drive.

5. If you are installing on a hard disk, enter a path for the PROCOMM PLUS home directory. For simplicity, use a path D:\PCPLUS\, where D is the letter for the drive that you want to use. Be careful not to skip over this step with this field set to a drive's root directory. Type **y** to create the directory, if it is new.

6. Enter your serial number, as it appears on your registration card (without any spaces).

7. Read the message onscreen and press the spacebar.

2 *Up & Running with PROCOMM PLUS*

STEP 1

8. Follow the directions onscreen that tell you to insert the distribution disks.

9. Read the message about CONFIG.SYS and AUTO-EXEC.BAT. Press any key *but* Esc to allow PCINSTAL to edit your system files—or press Esc and hand-edit your files, as you will read about later. Enter the root directory of your boot disk when prompted. If told that a file looks fine as is, press any key. When shown a proposed file modification at the bottom of the screen, type **y** to accept it or **n** to reject it. Press the spacebar when prompted.

Continue with the steps for adapting your copy of the program to your serial communications needs:

Adapting PROCOMM PLUS for your system

1. Highlight the appropriate choice for your system—to use PROCOMM PLUS with a modem only, with a direct connection to another computer only, or with both—and press Enter.

2. If you have chosen a direct connection only, choose (at successive following prompts) a serial port, a baud rate, and either "No parity, 8 data bits" or "Even parity, 7 data bits." You will be able to modify these choices later. You can then skip steps 3–7.

3. If you have chosen to use the program with a modem, read the message about setting up your modem.

4. Choose your default COM port by picking a number and pressing Enter.

5. Choose tone dialing or pulse dialing commands for your modem by typing the choice number and pressing Enter.

6. Read the note on choosing a type for your modem and press the spacebar.

7. Highlight your modem type using the keys listed on the screen. Pick a brand and type that your modem emulates, if necessary. (Many inexpensive modems emulate a Hayes Smartmodem [Hayes Microcomputer Products, Inc.] of a given speed.) Press Enter and wait while the program works.

Installation 3

STEP 1

8. Choose the file-transfer protocol that you use most often for downloads by typing the letter and pressing Enter. This choice is easily changed for particular services.
9. Enter a download path. You should designate a directory to be used exclusively to hold downloaded files. If the directory that you name does not yet exist, you can create it later.

Finishing the installation

The remaining steps confirm the success of your installation:

1. Read the message about PCINSTAL's report and press any key.
2. Browse through the report using the keys listed. Press Esc when you are done.
3. Type y when prompted to save a copy of the report. Press Enter to have it saved to the default file name.
4. Read the message about the Readme file and press any key.
5. Browse through the file as you did the previous report.
6. Read the final message and press any key to end the installation.

MODIFYING YOUR SYSTEM FILES

If you didn't allow PCINSTAL to modify your system files, you should do it yourself at this point. Use any text editor or word processor that can edit files in ASCII text (nondocument) mode to make the following changes to your system files.

Modifications to AUTOEXEC.BAT

Setting your path

Include your PROCOMM PLUS directory in your DOS path. For instance, if your AUTOEXEC.BAT contains a line reading

    path c:\dos;c:\wp

modify it to read

    path c:\dos;c:\wp;c:\pcplus

STEP 1

substituting the drive and directory that houses your PROCOMM PLUS files. If you have no path statement, add a line with the word *path* followed by a space and the complete path to your PROCOMM PLUS directory.

Also, add a line to the file that reads

    set pcplus=c:\pcplus\

again substituting your own drive and path.

Modifications to CONFIG.SYS

Make sure there is a line in your CONFIG.SYS file that reads

    files=25

Setting your files = line

(with a numerical value of at least 25). If there is no such line, add one to the file. After you exit your editor, reboot the computer to put these settings into effect.

Creating Your Download Directory

If the download directory that you named while running PCINSTAL does not exist, take a moment now to create it, using the DOS MD command.

SETTINGS FOR YOUR MODEM

As you noted while running PCINSTAL, certain modem settings are needed fully to integrate the modem and PROCOMM PLUS as a system. If your modem has a row of small switches, you should set two of them in particular. Consult your modem's documentation and set the corresponding switches so that the modem pays attention to the Data Terminal Ready (DTR) serial line and raises or lowers the Data Carrier Detect (DCD) line if another modem's carrier is detected or lost. On a Hayes-compatible modem, this means turning switches 1 and 6 on. If your modem has no switches, PROCOMM PLUS can make these settings with software commands, as explained later in Step 3.

Preparing your modem

Installation   5

STEP 2

Working with
PROCOMM PLUS

This Step teaches you a few basic operations for getting started with PROCOMM PLUS.

STARTING UP THE PROGRAM

Start PROCOMM PLUS from any directory by entering **pcplus** at the DOS command line. After the program has set some startup values and initialized your modem, it will offer you the prompt

    PRESS ANY KEY TO ENTER TERMINAL MODE

At this point, do as directed. You now arrive at the *terminal-mode screen*. This screen is the heart of PROCOMM PLUS—it is here that you type your messages to send to remote computers, or *remote systems,* and view their output. PROCOMM PLUS appropriates the bottom line of the screen as a status line to keep you informed of the state of your connection. Figure 2.1 shows the opening screen and names the elements of the status line. The following discussion provides a fuller description of their meanings.

The message box shows you current messages from PROCOMM PLUS about actions that it is performing. Most of the time, it displays a reminder that you can get context-sensitive help (descriptions of what you can do at a particular time) by pressing Alt-Z.

The message box

7

STEP 2

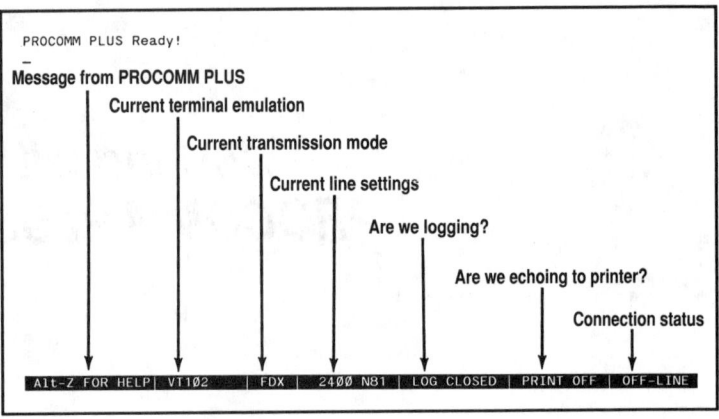

- *Figure 2.1: The terminal-mode screen*

The current terminal emulation

The current terminal-emulation box shows the type of computer terminal that your PC is currently emulating from the viewpoint of a remote system.

The current duplex mode

The current transmission-mode box reads "FDX" or "HDX." FDX (full duplex) means that PROCOMM PLUS assumes that what you type will be echoed, or retransmitted, by the remote system to your screen, to allow you to see your own typing. HDX (half duplex) means that PROCOMM PLUS itself will display your typing onscreen. You can switch between the two modes by pressing Alt-E.

Line settings

The current line-settings box shows your system's current communications rate in bits per second (often called the *baud rate*) and the settings for parity (N, O, E, M, or S for respective parity values of none, odd, even, mark, or space), the number of data bits, and the number of stop bits.

Log status

The message "LOG OPEN" in the file-log box tells you that your transactions with a remote system are currently being recorded in a log file for you to study later. The message "LOG CLOSED" tells you the contrary. You will learn how to use the log feature in Step 13.

The message "PRINT ON" in the print box tells you that your transactions are now being sent to a printer line-for-line. The message "PRINT OFF" tells you the contrary. This feature is also described in Step 13.

Printer status

The message "ON-LINE" in the connection-status box tells you that your modem is off-hook (in the same sense that a telephone can be off its hook) and exchanging carrier tones with a remote modem; thus it is connected with a remote system. The message "OFF-LINE" means the contrary. You go online by dialing and connecting with a remote system, as described in Step 5. You go offline by logging off that system and pressing Alt-H.

Connection status

INVOKING PROCOMM PLUS PROGRAM FUNCTIONS

PROCOMM PLUS provides two alternate means for invoking all of its setup and operational facilities. One is a Windows-style combination of menu bar and pulldown menus that you can invoke from the terminal-mode screen by pressing a hotkey. The other is a set of popup menu and entry screens that appear when you press a key while holding down the Alt key. After you read about each system in the next two sections, you can choose to learn whichever you find more convenient.

Using the Topline Menu

Bring up the topline menu by pressing `. Note that as you move across this menu by pressing ← or →, a pull-down menu appears. You can select an item from this menu by highlighting it (pressing ↑ or ↓, or by pressing the first letter of the name until it is highlighted) and pressing Enter. Some submenus lead to a further popup menu, as you can see if you select first Emulations and then VT/ANSI—the final menu level allows you to select a VT-series terminal to emulate, as shown in Figure 2.2.

For another example, highlight the leftmost item and press Enter to bring up the dialing directory, which will be described in Steps

Working with PROCOMM PLUS

STEP 2

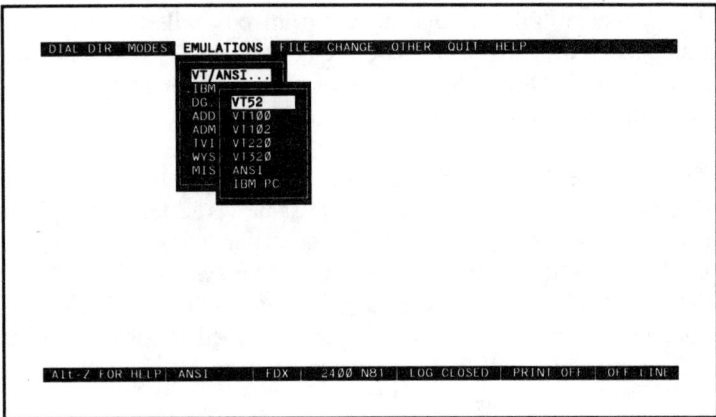

■ *Figure 2.2: The topline menu*

4 and 5. Press Esc to exit the directory and press ` to bring up the menu again. Bring up the first screen of the setup-menu system by highlighting CHANGE and pressing Enter with the first item, SETUP, highlighted. Press Esc to exit. Setup menus are further described below.

Using the Alt-Key Method

Press Alt-Z now from the terminal-mode screen to see the PRO-COMM PLUS command-summary screen shown in Figure 2.3. You can press Alt-Z from most points within PROCOMM PLUS to get context-sensitive help. In this case, the first press of this key combination brings up the command-summary screen, which shows each program function available from the terminal-mode screen, together with the key combination that invokes it. (Note, for instance, under the heading "SET UP" that you can bring up the setup facility by pressing Alt-S from the terminal screen, just as you brought it up through the topline menu.)

The second press of Alt-Z gives you extended information about the terminal-mode screen, which consists of explanations of the terminal mode, the status line, the help system, and the terminal emulation. You can move through the help system by pressing the keys listed at the bottom of the screen. For instance, you can move

10 *Up & Running with PROCOMM PLUS*

through the help screen with ↑, ↓, PgUp, or PgDn, and you can change topics by pressing **t**, highlighting a new topic, and pressing Enter. You can search for text under a topic by pressing **s** and entering search text. To search for the next instance of the text, press **c**. Press Esc twice to return to the terminal-mode screen itself.

CHANGING PROCOMM PLUS SETTINGS

Press Alt-S from the terminal-mode screen to bring up the first setup screen. As with the topline menu, you can choose from among these menu items by highlighting one and pressing Enter, or by pressing an item's first letter.

Setting Miscellaneous Values

Press **d** now for Display/Sound Options, a set of items that affect the program's display. Then press Alt-Z for brief descriptions of the items appearing on this menu. Again, you can page through them by pressing PgUp or PgDn. Press Esc to return to the menu and then press **b** to choose item B, Sound Effects. The status line now includes the message

Display options

```
Press space to toggle, ↵ to accept
```

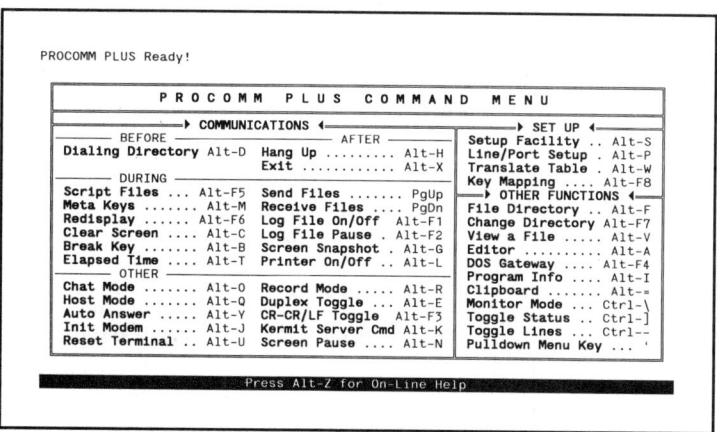

- *Figure 2.3: The command-summary menu*

Working with PROCOMM PLUS **11**

STEP 2

Sound effects

This is typical of menu items with a fixed set of possible values, among which you choose by pressing the spacebar. The Sound Effects item controls whether the program signals the display and removal of windows with whistling notes. If you need quiet at your workstation, press the spacebar and then Enter to accept "OFF" as the new setting. Otherwise, press Esc.

Note that other settings require you to enter a numerical value after you select them; these have appropriate messages in the status line. For instance, press **d** to choose item D, Alarm Time. The status line reads as follows:

```
Enter a number from 0 to 9999 and press ↵
```

The alarm sounds whenever PROCOMM PLUS needs to get your attention, as when a file transfer is concluded. If you wish the alarm to sound for more or fewer seconds than the number shown, type in the number and press Enter. Otherwise, press Esc to leave the old value in place. Press Esc again to return to the main setup screen.

Editing Long Entries

You will often have reason to make text entries while using PROCOMM PLUS, such as names of files to be transferred—sometimes including paths to the DOS directories where they reside. PROCOMM PLUS offers a consistent system for entering and editing such entries, in any context within the program. Table 2.1 shows the keystrokes available to you on these occasions.

Key	Function
←	Moves the cursor left across characters
→	Moves the cursor right across characters
Home	Moves the cursor to the start of the line
End	Moves the cursor to the right end of the line

Table 2.1: PROCOMM PLUS Editing Keys

Key	Function
Backspace	Deletes the character to the left of the cursor
Delete	Deletes the character over the cursor
Insert	Toggles between inserting characters before the character at the cursor (shown by a tall cursor) and overwriting the character at the cursor (shown by a short cursor)
Tab	Advances the cursor directly to the next field
Shift-Tab	Moves the cursor to the previous field
Ctrl-Backspace	Deletes the current line
Ctrl-End	Deletes the line from the cursor to the right end of the field
Esc	Leaves the line, abandoning changes
Enter	Leaves the line, incorporating changes

Table 2.1: PROCOMM PLUS Editing Keys (continued)

From the opening setup screen, press **f** to bring up the File/Path Options menu. Note option C—"Default path for downloaded files (PgDn)." The entry should match the choice that you made when you installed PROCOMM PLUS. If you want to change this setting, press **c**, type in the new path, edit it using the keystrokes shown in the table, and press Enter when you are done.

Keep downloaded files together

Saving Setup Values

There are two ways to save the new settings that you have made. Return to the first setup screen by pressing Esc. From here, press **s** (for SAVE SETUP OPTIONS) and press Esc to return to the terminal-mode screen. (Wherever you are in PROCOMM PLUS, you can always return to the terminal-mode screen by pressing Esc one or more times.)

If you have made changes to your setup but do not save them in this way, PROCOMM PLUS will prompt you on your way back to

Working with PROCOMM PLUS

STEP 2

the terminal mode:

MAKE CHANGES PERMANENT? (Y/N)

You can then save the settings to disk by pressing **y**.

THE LINE/PORT SETUP MENU

You should become acquainted with the menu that sets your communications rate and parity, as well as the serial port that you are using. Bring up this menu, shown in Figure 2.4, by pressing Alt-P from the terminal-mode screen.

Your current settings are shown on the top line of the menu. To make a setting, press the letter key, number key, function key, or Alt-key combination shown to the left of the desired setting. For instance, press **4** to set your communications rate to 4,800 bits per second, or press F2 to make COM2 your current serial port. Note that you can quickly set two very common sets of data bit/parity values: 8 data bits with no parity or 7 data bits with even parity, by pressing Alt-N or Alt-E, respectively.

```
PROCOMM PLUS Ready!

                    CURRENT SETTINGS:   2400,N,8,1,COM1

         BAUD RATE    PARITY       DATA BITS    STOP BITS    PORT

         1)    300    N) NONE      Alt-7) 7     Alt-1) 1     F1) COM1
         2)   1200    E) EVEN      Alt-8) 8     Alt-2) 2     F2) COM2
         3)   2400    O) ODD                                 F3) COM3
         4)   4800    M) MARK                                F4) COM4
         5)   9600    S) SPACE                               F5) COM5
         6)  19200                                           F6) COM6
         7)  38400                                           F7) COM7
         8)  57600    Alt-N) N/8/1                           F8) COM8
         9) 115200    Alt-E) E/7/1

         Esc) Exit    Alt-S) Save and Exit    YOUR CHOICE: _


                              LINE/PORT SETUP
```

■ *Figure 2.4: The line/port setup menu*

Your settings take effect immediately. To save them to disk, press Alt-S. They will then be in force every time you start PROCOMM PLUS. To leave this menu, press Esc. Note that all of these values may be overridden by settings for the dialing-directory entries described in Step 4.

EXITING PROCOMM PLUS

To leave PROCOMM PLUS, press Alt-X at the terminal-mode screen. A window appears in the upper-left corner of the screen asking you to confirm your choice. Press **y** to return to DOS.

If you are online at this point, PROCOMM PLUS displays a second window asking whether you want to hang up. Press **y** for PROCOMM PLUS to instruct your modem to hang up. Otherwise, you are returned to DOS while still online.

Checking Your Setup

The information in this step allows you to make sure that your communications setup is fully operational.

COMMUNICATING WITH YOUR MODEM

For the most part, PROCOMM PLUS takes over the job of communicating with your modem, sending it commands and receiving responses over the lines leading from your computer's serial port. You should be aware of how some of this interaction works to be sure that the program is set properly for your modem.

Bring up the Modem Command Options menu shown in Figure 3.1 by pressing Alt-S, **m**, and then **m** again from the terminal-mode screen. The values shown in the figure are those appropriate for a Hayes-compatible modem.

Take a look, for instance, at option A, the Initialization command. This line of characters is normally sent to your modem every time you start PROCOMM PLUS. Each sequence of two to six characters here has a special meaning to the modem, which you can learn about by perusing your modem's manual. For instance, the AT sequence signals the beginning of a command to the modem.

The modem initialization sequence

STEP 3

```
PROCOMM PLUS SETUP UTILITY                    MODEM COMMAND OPTIONS
   A- Initialization command .. ATE1Q0V1X4&C1&D2 S7=60 S11=55 S0=0^M
   B- Dialing command ......... ATDT
   C- Dialing command suffix .. ^M
   D- Hangup command .......... ~~~+++~~~AT H0^M
   E- Auto answer on command .. ~~~+++~~~ATS0=1^M
   F- Auto answer off command . ~~~+++~~~ATS0=0^M




   Alt Z: Help    Press the letter of the option to change    Esc: Exit
```

■ *Figure 3.1: The Modem Command Options menu*

Note the two sequences &C1 and &D2. These two commands are equivalent in effect to the two switch settings discussed in Step 1; that is, &C1 tells the modem to signal the computer when a remote carrier is detected or lost through the DCD serial line, and &D2 tells the modem to hang up and ready itself for fresh commands when the computer signals "not ready" through the DTR line. The sequence ^M at the end of the string means to send a carriage return, which signals the end of a command to a Hayes-compatible modem.

Your modem's manual describes these and other commands that deal with conditions you may encounter. For instance, the X4 command sets up your modem to dial only when it detects a dial tone, to recognize and announce busy signals, and to announce the transmission speed of its connection with the remote system. If you have a dial tone too weak for the modem to detect, you can edit the command to read "X3," which allows dialing in the absence of a dial tone. You can change this line by pressing **a**, editing it using the keys listed in the previous step, and pressing Enter.

The dialing command sequence

Option B, the Dialing command, is a sequence that precedes any telephone number in your dialing directory. DT means "tone dial";

if you need pulse dialing, you can edit this line to read "DP." If you are connected to a PBX system, you can edit this line to read "ATDT9W" to connect to an outside line and wait for a second dial tone.

Call waiting

You can also use this feature to turn off *call waiting* before any call. This telephone company service, which announces that a caller is trying to reach you while you are on the line, briefly interrupts your connection, and so can cause your modem to lose the remote carrier. If you have call waiting, edit option B to read "ATDT*70," to suspend the service before every call. The comma tells the modem to pause briefly before dialing the digits of the telephone number. Consult your telephone directory or company for the exact sequence to turn off call waiting in your area.

Other modem and serial port settings

Exit the Modem Command Options menu by pressing Esc. The other three menus available from this level also deal with communicating with your modem, but they rarely need to be changed. The General Options menu includes several settings pertaining to the timing and control of serial lines for special hardware configurations. The Result Messages menu tells PROCOMM PLUS what messages to expect from the modem to signify connection at various transmission speeds, or to signify a failure to connect. The Port Assignments menu specifies details of how your system addresses your serial port, specifications that are standard in most instances. Press Esc twice more (and type y when prompted if you've made any changes that you want to save) to return to the terminal-mode screen.

If you made any changes to your modem's initialization sequence, exit and restart PROCOMM PLUS with the modem running and connected so that they will take effect.

CHECKING IN WITH YOUR MODEM

At the terminal-mode screen, make sure that you are in full duplex mode (as shown by the letters "FDX" on the status line). Enter **AT** or substitute the command prefix for your own modem if it is not Hayes-compatible. Most modems of recent manufacture also accept

Checking Your Setup 19

commands in lowercase letters. The letters "AT" themselves should appear onscreen, meaning that the modem has echoed them back, and the modem should respond on the next line with the message "OK," meaning that it has carried out the command successfully.

If the Modem Doesn't Respond...

If you have an external modem, make sure that it is turned on and connected to your serial port. Press Alt-H (for both external and built-in modems); this sends the hangup command (option D of the Modem Command Options menu) to your modem and assures that it is ready to respond to commands. Now send the AT command again.

If you are not sure which serial port your modem is connected to, bring up the Line/Port Setup menu by pressing Alt-P. If PROCOMM PLUS is currently set to use, say, COM1, press F2 to change the setting to COM2. Press Esc and repeat the test above. You can try the other COM ports in this way.

If you see any extraneous characters onscreen, some other serial device may be interfering with your modem. Correcting this may require changing serial ports or IRQ lines. The latter are beyond the scope of this book, but you should consult the manuals for both PROCOMM PLUS and your modem or serial card before making a choice. You can make the new setting effective in PROCOMM PLUS through the Port Assignments menu described previously.

When the modem responds correctly, you can be assured that your system is fully functional.

STEP 4

Using the Dialing Directory

This Step acquaints you with the important skills of navigating and editing the PROCOMM PLUS dialing directory, which you use to dial remote systems from your computer.

CHOOSING A DIALING DIRECTORY

From the PROCOMM PLUS terminal-mode screen, press Alt-D to bring up the Dialing Directory window. The name of the default directory, PCPLUS.DIR, appears on the top line. The first ten entries (out of 200 total) are displayed underneath, followed by a listing of usable keystrokes with their meanings, a prompt for an action, and the status line. As supplied in a new installation, this directory is blank, waiting for you to fill in some entries. Before you do this, you should learn to work with a directory that already includes real entries.

The Dialing Directory window

Press Esc to return to the terminal-mode screen for the moment. PROCOMM PLUS comes supplied with several sample dialing directories, each including entries for bulletin boards and other services in a given area of the United States. These directories are included on your supplemental disk; each has the standard dialing directory extension .DIR. You can list them now using the program's built-in file-listing facility.

STEP 4

Entering a file spec

Press Alt-F and a window appears prompting you for a *file spec*, that is, a file name or a name that uses the wildcard * or ? to define a set of files. Enter the path to your PROCOMM PLUS home directory (established by the SET PCPLUS= command), followed by a file spec to list all files with the extension .DIR, like this:

    c:\pcplus*.dir

You will see a listing like that shown in Figure 4.1. In addition to the default directory, directories for different regions of the U.S. will appear.

You can remove this listing by pressing any key.

If you call for a listing of more files than fit in a window, the legend "–MORE–" appears at the bottom. Successive keystrokes will then show you further screenfuls of files until the listing is exhausted.

WORKING WITH A DIALING DIRECTORY

At this point, press Escape to exit the dialing-directory display. Return to the dialing directory by pressing Alt-D. The command to

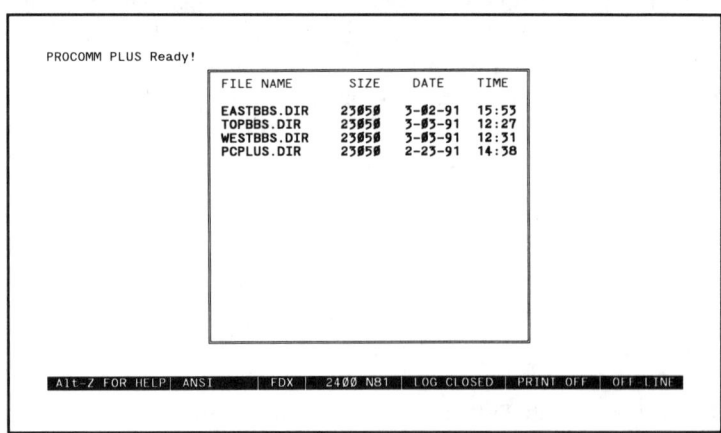

- *Figure 4.1: Listing of available dialing directories*

22 *Up & Running with PROCOMM PLUS*

load a new directory is **x**, mnemonic for "exchange directory." Press this key and, at the entry window, type in the name **topbbs** and press Enter. Note that there is no need for the file extension, and in fact there is no room to add it. The new directory will appear, as shown in Figure 4.2.

Getting Around in the Directory

Any dialing directory consists of 200 entries, including blank entries. These keystrokes move you from point to point within a directory:

Directory navigation

- Press Home to go to the first ten entries of a directory (beginning with entry 1). Press End to go to the last ten entries (beginning with entry 191).

- Press PgUp or PgDn to move backward or forward, respectively, one screenful of ten entries. At the end of the directory, PgDn returns you to the top. Similarly, PgUp takes you from the first screenful of entries to the last.

- Press ↑ or ↓ to highlight the previous or next entry. When you reach the top or bottom of a screenful of entries, ↑ highlights the last entry on the previous screen, while ↓ highlights the first entry on the next screen, respectively.

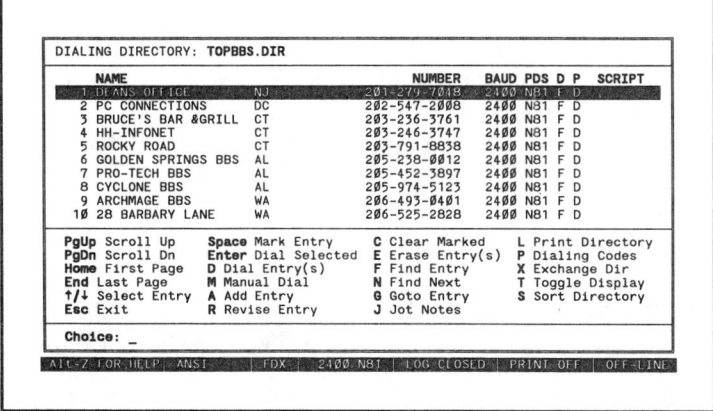

- *Figure 4.2: The TOPBBS directory*

Using the Dialing Directory

STEP 4

Going Directly to an Entry

If you know an entry by number, press **g** for Goto and enter that number. The corresponding entry will be highlighted.

Searching for a Sequence of Characters

When you forget the exact entry

If you remember part of a service's name or telephone number, you can use it to search for the service. For instance, press **f** for Find, type in **bbs**, and press Enter to find the first occurrence of the characters "bbs" in a name (whether they are upper- or lowercase). You can then find further instances by successive presses of **n** for Find Next. The search wraps; that is, once it has reached entry 200, it continues with entry 1.

For another example, try pressing **f**, entering **303-**, and then pressing **n** once or twice to find all telephone numbers beginning with "303-."

Printing a Directory

You can print a directory by pressing **l** ("el," not "one") and entering the name of your printing port. If the printer is connected to your computer's first parallel port (PRN), you can just press Enter when the prompt window appears. Otherwise, type in the port name, press Enter for the narrow format, and press Enter to start.

You can also "print" the directory to a file (in printed format) by entering a file name in place of the device name. The directory will be printed 50 entries to a page, with page breaks and identifying headers and footers. All 200 entries will be printed, including blank entries.

Erasing Entries

You can erase an entry by highlighting it and pressing **e** for Erase. You will see a prompt similar to the following:

    ERASE ENTRY NUMBER 17? (Y/N)

Press y to confirm.

You can also mark several entries and delete them at once. To mark an entry, highlight it and press the spacebar. A wedge-shaped character appears in the left margin. To unmark the entry, highlight it and press the spacebar again. To unmark all marked entries, press c.

Try scrolling to some unused entries and marking three of them in this way. Press e. You will be prompted as follows:

    ERASE 3 MARKED ENTRIES? (Y/N)

If you press y, the entries will be erased. If you press n, you will be prompted to erase the highlighted entry, as described above. The erased entries will not be overwritten by later entries but will remain blank.

This process of marking entries is also used to choose entries to dial, as you will learn about in Step 5.

Sorting a Directory

You can sort your directory entries by any of several criteria. From the directory window, press first s for Sort and then n, p, b, t, or l to sort by name, telephone number, communications rate, total number of calls, or date of last call, respectively. Sorting takes a moment. Any of these methods of sorting eliminates gaps left by previous deletions among your active entries.

Making Notes

You can write a quick note on an entry while perusing a dialing directory. To jot a note, press j. Enter a name for the note file when prompted. This function calls PCEDIT, the text editor provided with PROCOMM PLUS (described in Step 9) or else the editor that you have designated (as described in Step 18). In the case of PCEDIT, you can save your note, leave the editor, and return to the dialing directory by pressing Alt-X.

Using the Dialing Directory

STEP 4

WORKING WITH DIRECTORY ENTRIES

As you see, each entry represents a service that you can dial. Generally, you will be making your own entries for contacting the online services of your choice, as you will do later in this Step.

What a Directory Entry Means

Reading from left to right, the directory contains the entry number, the name that you use for the service, its telephone number, and the communications rate in bits per second (baud), parity, data bits, stop bits, and duplex mode (full or half) that you use to communicate with it. The next-to-last column shows the number of the serial-port setting for this entry. Entries are initially set to the default port that you chose during installation, designated by the letter *D*. The last column, SCRIPT, designates a file in which you can record the steps that you take to log onto that service, to be performed automatically. You will read about script files in Steps 15 and 16.

Press t to see an alternate screen of directory information. On this screen, besides the entry number and name, you see PROCOMM PLUS's record of the number of times that you have called that entry and the date you last called it (which should all be zeros for a new installation), as well as your chosen terminal type and file transfer protocol. Press t a second time to see the mode of connection (MODEM or DIRECT) for the entries onscreen, as well as the Meta file (basically a set of keyboard macros, see Step 14), the Kbd file (a file for mapping the keyboard), and the note file (described above) that may be associated with any of them. Press t a third time to return to the original display.

How to Create a Directory Entry

Creating a dialing directory

To prepare to create some entries, create a new dialing directory by pressing x and entering a name for your directory, for instance, new. Notice that the transmission speed, parity, data bits, stop bits, duplex mode, file transfer protocol, and terminal emulation for all entries are set to the values that you chose as you installed the

26 *Up & Running with PROCOMM PLUS*

program. This speeds the entry of your most frequently used values, but you can easily substitute others for any given entry.

To add a new directory entry, press **a**. A window appears that accepts information to fill the first blank entry in the directory. (To revise an existing entry, highlight it and press **r**—the process from that point on is the same as that for a new entry.) To create an entry for CompuServe (CompuServe, Inc.), follow these steps below. (You need only press Enter to accept a value that already appears correctly.)

Adding entries to it

1. Type in the name **CompuServe** and press Enter.
2. Enter your local CompuServe phone number. To get it, call them at 1-800-635-6225 (by telephone). Note that you can add parentheses, hyphens, and spaces to the field for readability. If you don't have a number on hand now, enter a dummy number for practice.
3. Enter the communications rate by highlighting it in the popup window and pressing Enter. Use your modem's highest speed or the highest rate of the communications link, whichever is lower.
4. Similarly, choose EVEN parity from the window that appears.
5. Press Enter to leave DATA BITS at 7.
6. Press Enter to leave STOP BITS at 1.
7. Highlight FULL for duplex and press Enter.
8. Press Enter to leave PORT at DEFAULT.
9. Press Enter to skip the SCRIPT field.
10. Highlight COMPUSERVE B+ and press Enter to choose the CompuServe B file-transfer protocol.
11. Highlight VT/ANSI, press Enter, highlight ANSI for your terminal type, and press Enter.
12. Bypass the remaining fields in this window by pressing Enter for each. Successively, they allow you to associate a

STEP 4

password (for use in a script), a Meta file, a keyboard mapping file, and a note file with this entry.

13. If the entry looks right, press Enter to retain the existing date and totals (useful on old entries you are revising).

14. Press Enter again to accept the entry. (If you are not satisfied with it, press **n**. You will be returned to the NAME field so that you can begin editing the entry.)

15. At this point, your screen should resemble Figure 4.3. Press Enter once again to make the new entry permanent.

Using Dialing Codes

Save time dialing

When a series of digits occurs in many of the numbers that you dial, you can include it in a *dialing code,* which you then represent in a given entry as a single letter. Suppose, for instance, you are calling several 800 numbers:

1. Press **p** for Dialing Codes to bring up the dialing codes menu. Note that entries A through J exist.

2. With entry A highlighted, press **r** for Revise.

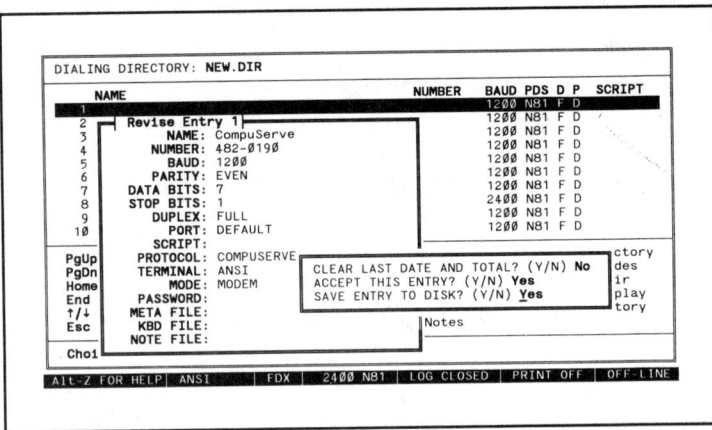

- *Figure 4.3: The CompuServe entry*

28 *Up & Running with PROCOMM PLUS*

STEP 4

3. Assuming that you must preface 800 numbers with the digit 1, type in **1 (800)** and press Enter.
4. Press Esc to leave the window.
5. Move down a line in the dialing directory and create an entry for MCI mail, which has an 800 number, as follows:

```
      NAME:  MCI Mail
    NUMBER:  A234-6245
      BAUD:  2400 [or whatever is applicable]
    PARITY:  N
 DATA BITS:  8
 STOP BITS:  1
    DUPLEX:  FULL
      PORT:  DEFAULT
    SCRIPT:
  PROTOCOL:  ASCII
  TERMINAL:  ANSI
```

6. Leave the remaining fields blank as before and save these values as you did for the preceding entry.

Now whenever you dial MCI mail, the area code will be substituted automatically for the letter *A*. Dialing codes can be placed anywhere they are needed within a telephone number.

With this preparation, you are ready to dial out and go online.

Dialing Remote Systems

In this Step, you have the chance to dial out and make contact with the world outside. You will learn about the various ways to dial with PROCOMM PLUS and try conversing with another user.

CIRCULAR DIALING

In a circular dial, you choose two or more services that you would like to reach and then PROCOMM PLUS tries each in turn, repeatedly, until it connects with one. When you are finished with that service, you can return to the dialing directory and retry the remaining entries. This feature is a great boon, because many on-line services are difficult to reach, having busy phone lines much of the time.

Dialing multiple services

You can read through this section as a thought experiment, or you can make entries for services that you would like to reach and try these techniques on them. If you work with one of the sample directories as shown in the examples, first remove the area codes from entries that you call, if they are local numbers.

For instance, bring up the dialing directory by pressing Alt-D from the PROCOMM PLUS terminal-mode screen. To use the TOPBBS sample directory, press **x**, type **topbbs**, and press Enter.

STEP 5

Enumerating entries to dial

Suppose you want to contact each of the first three services that appear in this directory. (Note that they have been edited to add a long-distance dialing prefix.) You can designate entries to dial in either of two ways. To try the first method, press **d** for dial. Type the numbers **1 2 3** into the entry window, separated by spaces. Press Enter to begin dialing. Press Esc to abort the dial so that you can try the alternate method.

Marking entries to dial

For the second method, mark the first three entries as you marked entries to erase in Step 4, by highlighting each in turn and pressing the spacebar. When you have marked the entries, press Enter.

In either case, when you press Enter, PROCOMM PLUS begins dialing the first entry and the dialing window appears, as shown in Figure 5.1. This window keeps you posted on the status of the current round of dialing and allows you to change certain settings. First, consider the fields in the window:

The fields described

- DIALING: the entry name now being dialed
- NUMBER: the telephone number now being dialed
- SCRIPT: the script file that will be run upon connection, if you have associated one with this entry

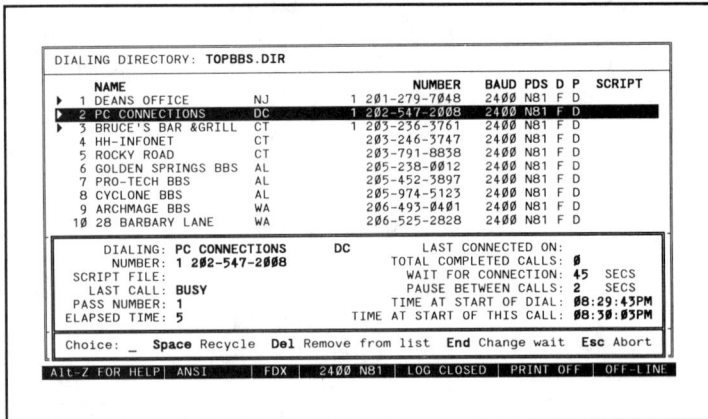

- *Figure 5.1: The Dialing window*

32 *Up & Running with PROCOMM PLUS*

STEP 5

- LAST CALL: the result of the last call. For instance, BUSY means the line was busy, and TIMEOUT may mean that the line kept ringing with no answer until the allotted time was exhausted (see the items WAIT FOR CONNECTION and End below) or that the call was not completed by that time

- PASS NUMBER: a pass includes one try of each of the entries chosen for a round of circular dialing

- ELAPSED TIME: how many seconds since PROCOMM PLUS began dialing this number in this pass

- LAST CONNECTED ON: the date that you last reached an entry, as shown on the alternate directory screen

- TOTAL COMPLETED CALLS: how many times you have reached this entry, also shown on the alternate directory screen

- WAIT FOR CONNECTION: how many seconds to let elapse without a connection before moving on to the next entry (the initial wait time is set in the Modem General Options menu)

- PAUSE BETWEEN CALLS: how many seconds to wait between dropping one dial attempt and trying the next entry on the list; your modem may need a brief pause to reset (the value is set in the Modem General Options menu)

- TIME AT START OF DIAL: the time at which you pressed Enter to begin dialing and the dialing window appeared

- TIME AT START OF THIS CALL: the time that the modem last went off hook and began dialing this entry

Now regard the choices on the bottom line of the dialing window: *Your choices*

- Space: by pressing the spacebar, you stop dialing the current entry and move on to the next one chosen

- Del: by pressing Del, you abandon your attempt to reach the current entry during this round of dialing; PROCOMM PLUS removes it from the list, stops dialing it, and moves on to the next entry

Dialing Remote Systems 33

- End: after pressing End, you are prompted to enter the number of seconds that PROCOMM PLUS will wait for a connection before moving on to the next entry; your new value takes effect at once and remains in effect until you exit PROCOMM PLUS or enter yet another value

- Esc: by pressing Esc, you cancel the current round of dialing, remove the dialing window, and return to the dialing directory

If you get repeated "TIMEOUT" messages next to LAST CALL, try turning on your modem's speaker (if it is not already on) to find out what is happening. Cancel the dial and leave the dialing directory by pressing Esc twice. Turn on the speaker by entering the command **ATM1** (in the case of Hayes-compatible modems) at the terminal-mode screen. Resume your dialing as before. Now you can hear what the problem is: you may hear ringing signals, or a recorded voice telling you that a number has been changed or disconnected. Alternatively, dial the number with a telephone and listen. If you hear a voice message, jot down any useful information. If you hear a tone, you may have to use commands to adjust values stored in some of your modem's S registers to allow it to detect your carrier. See your modem's documentation for more information.

Dialing a Single Entry

To dial a single entry, clear any existing markings, highlight the desired entry, and press Enter. Recall that you press **c** to clear markings. (You will try this procedure in Step 6.)

Connecting

When PROCOMM PLUS connects with a service, it sounds a beeping alarm and removes the dialing window and the dialing-directory window. You are returned to the terminal-mode screen connected with the service. PROCOMM PLUS prints a one-line message at the top of the terminal screen:

    PROCOMM PLUS online to Service at Rate

For *Service* it inserts the name entry that you supplied. *Rate* is the actual communications rate of the achieved connection.

MANUAL DIALING AND A LOOK AT CHAT MODE

For this exercise, find a friend or associate who has a computer, modem, and communications program—as well as a few minutes to spare. He or she should run the communications program with the modem set up in *auto-answer* mode so that the modem answers a ringing signal. In PROCOMM PLUS, this is done by pressing Alt-Y from the terminal-mode screen. Once you have started PROCOMM PLUS, set your systems to the same communications rate and parity.

Bring up the dialing directory by pressing Alt-D, then press **m** for manual dial. The manual dialing feature is handy when you want to try a number on an ad hoc basis without going through the formalities of making an entry. Type in your friend's telephone number and press Enter.

Manual dialing

As PROCOMM PLUS dials, it displays a dialing window as it does for a circular dial. Since there is no entry name, the DIALING field simply reads **MANUAL DIAL**.

When you connect, the beeping alarm sounds and the dialing window as well as the dialing directory disappear, leaving you at the terminal screen. If your friend types a message, you should see it onscreen. If you type something, it will probably not be echoed by the remote communications program. (This is an example of half-duplex operation.)

Instead of pressing Alt-E to turn on local echo, take this step to help organize the proceedings: Press Alt-O to start chat mode. PROCOMM PLUS reorganizes the screen to resemble Figure 5.2. What your friend types appears in the upper window of the screen and what you type appears in the lower window. PROCOMM PLUS will not send a line of your prose until you press Enter, so

Chat mode

you can remove mistakes by backspacing and retyping before they become public. (Option N in the Setup General Options menu determines whether your typing is sent by the line or by the character.) You can return to terminal mode by pressing Esc. You must leave chat mode in this way before conducting an operation like a file transfer or before hanging up. Therefore, when you run out of things to say, enter something like **Bye now,** press Esc, and then press Alt-H to hang up.

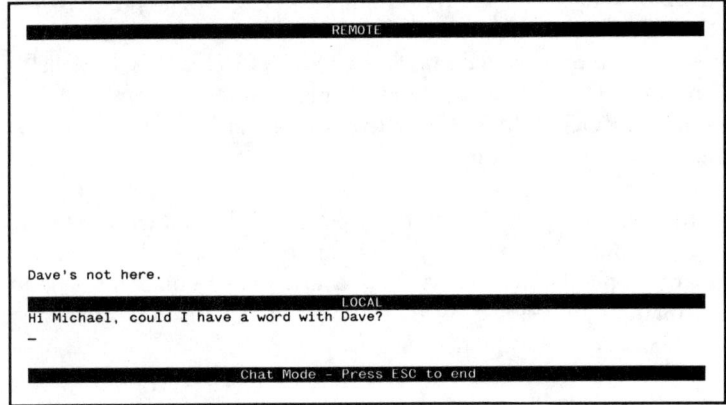

- *Figure 5.2: Chat mode*

Going Online

STEP 6

If you are new to online communications, learning to use PRO-COMM PLUS may be only half the battle—you must also learn to navigate an online service. This Step introduces you to the popular service called CompuServe (CompuServe, Inc.), which has an inexpensive monthly base rate and allows you to cancel your account whenever you like. You also learn how to make a log file that records your transactions while you are online.

Specific menu items and other aspects of online services do change over time. As you try out the examples below, be observant and make sure that you choose the items matching the descriptions in the text, regardless of their numbers.

SIGNING UP FOR COMPUSERVE

To sign up for CompuServe, have your introductory membership booklet and a credit card number on hand. Make sure that your modem is turned on and connected. Start PROCOMM PLUS and bring up the dialing directory by pressing Alt-D. Switch to your new dialing directory by pressing **x** and entering the directory name **new**.

With the CompuServe entry highlighted, press Enter to begin dialing. You are going to make a log file to create a record of your

Making the log file

37

STEP 6

Logging on

initial CompuServe session. When you are connected and have returned to the terminal screen, press Alt-F1 to open a log file. Enter **firstlog** to name the new log. Note that the status line now contains the message "LOG OPEN."

Press Enter, if necessary, to trigger the remote system to send the Host Name prompt. At that prompt, enter **cis** or the host name given in the introductory booklet. At successive prompts, enter the temporary user name, password, agreement number, and serial number given in the booklet. Note that the password is not echoed—though as an aid to typing, you can make it visible by pressing Alt-E before and after typing it. If you are opening a new account, provide answers to all of the questions that follow in the format requested. In the course of these questions, you will be given a permanent ID and a new temporary password, which will appear in your log file. You should thus preserve this file and keep it private. (You will be sent a permanent password later through the U. S. mail.) When you have completed your registration, you see a menu like this:

```
Please select

1 Online Tour (FREE)
2 Practice Forum (FREE)
3 CompuServe Information Service

Key choice:
```

To make a choice, enter the corresponding digit. For instance, for CompuServe itself, enter **3**. You should soon see the service's top menu, shown in Figure 6.1.

NAVIGATING COMPUSERVE

Compu-Serve described

CompuServe is organized as a branching system of menus such as the one before you. Note its features:

- The name of the menu screen itself, which appears in the upper-right corner. This menu is named "TOP"

38 *Up & Running with PROCOMM PLUS*

```
CompuServe                                              TOP


  1 Member Assistance (FREE)
  2 Find a Topic (FREE)
  3 Communications/Bulletin Bds.
  4 News/Weather/Sports
  5 Travel
  6 The Electronic MALL/Shopping
  7 Money Matters/Markets
  8 Entertainment/Games
  9 Hobbies/Lifestyles/Education
 10 Reference
 11 Computers/Technology
 12 Business/Other Interests



Enter choice number !_
 Alt-Z FOR HELP | ANSI   | FDX  | 1200 E71 | LOG CLOSED | PRINT OFF | ON-LINE
```

- *Figure 6.1: The CompuServe TOP menu*

   - A list of choices (many themselves submenus) consisting of a number and a description

   - The prompt "Enter choice !" (or some variation) followed by the cursor

You can enter any of several commands at the ! prompt to accomplish your task. Here are the most important commands that you can use:

Important commands to know

   - Enter the number of one of the items to move to a menu one level lower or to carry out that task. You will see an example in a moment.

   - Enter **m** to back up to the next higher menu.

   - Enter **t** to back up to the main menu of a CompuServe entity such as a forum. If you are already at a forum main menu or at a general system menu, entering **t** takes you back to the TOP menu that you see now.

   - Enter **go** *name* to jump to the menu called *name*. You will see an example later in this Step.

   - Enter **find** *name* to find menus that refer to *name*.

   - Enter **bye** to log off CompuServe.

STEP 6

- Enter **h** for help to see a summary of commands available at this prompt. You can also learn about commands available in particular situations this way.

Choosing Menus by Their Number

Note that the first two items on the TOP menu are marked FREE, meaning that you incur no connect charges while in a submenu under these items. Try entering the digit **1** for Member Assistance. Note that the next submenu, HELP, offers several further choices such as information on billing and telephone access numbers. Enter **4** to reach the MEMBER menu, which allows you to make changes to your account. For instance, choice 4 allows you to turn on or off the Executive Option, which gives you access to certain business services at a substantially raised monthly fee. For now, however, enter **5** to change your equipment/display profile, then **2** to change your permanent settings, **4** to select terminal type/parameters, and finally **1** to see a list of available terminal types. At this point, your choice will actually perform an action—that of informing CompuServe what kind of display terminal your software is emulating. Enter **2** to choose an ANSI terminal (the terminal you chose for the CompuServe dialing-directory entry). Press Enter to return to the preceding menu. Note that CompuServe begins writing menus more crisply than before.

At this point, you could enter **m** several times to return to the TOP menu, but instead, just enter **t**. You will be asked whether you want your changed setting to be made permanent; enter **1** to assent.

Choosing a Service by Its Name

If you want to find the CompuServe forum operated by Datastorm Technologies, Inc., the makers of PROCOMM PLUS, enter the command

    find datastorm

at the prompt. CompuServe responds with

    1 DATASTORM Forum   [DATASTORM]

This means that CompuServe found the word "Datastorm" once—in the name of a forum called DATASTORM, which you can reach by entering **go** followed by the keyword between square brackets on the right (in this case, DATASTORM again).

COMPUSERVE FORUMS

Forums allow people with varied interests to chat, exchange messages, and upload or download relevant files. Some hardware or software manufacturers, such as Datastorm, maintain forums to provide technical support and to disseminate updates and other material.

Once you have read the introductory matter (pressing Enter after each screen) and have reached the main menu as shown in Figure 6.2, type **8** and press Enter to join the forum. You incur no extra charges or obligations. Enter your name in upper- and lowercase letters.

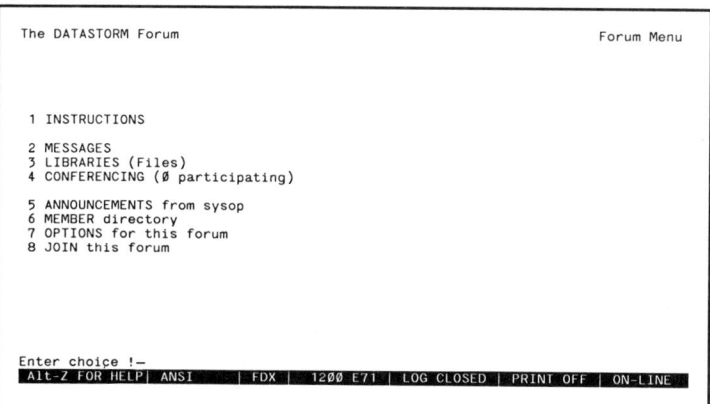

- *Figure 6.2: A forum main menu*

As an example of what forums offer, enter **2** to choose the MESSAGES menu. The following menu allows you to perform certain operations, such as selecting messages by subject or reading new messages that may be directed to you. If, for instance, you enter **1** for SELECT, you will find that item 3 on the next menu deals with PROCOMM PLUS. By entering **3**, you will see screenfuls of active topics that you can select by number. When you select a topic, you are shown the messages themselves; you may reply to any one message (after entering **choices**), skip to the next message (by pressing Enter), or return to the preceding menu (by entering **m**).

You can enter **3** to choose LIBRARIES (Files) from the main forum menu to browse through descriptions of files to download. You will read more about this option in the next Step.

LEAVING COMPUSERVE

Exit the service by entering **bye** at any ! prompt. When the initial Host Name prompt reappears, you are logged off the service and may safely press Alt-H to hang up the line or press Alt-X to exit PROCOMM PLUS. The program automatically closes your log file before exiting, and you can edit or print it as a record of your session by invoking the PRINT command at the DOS prompt:

    c:>print firstlog

To close the log in mid-session, press Alt-F1. The LOG CLOSED message will appear on the status line.

Receiving a File

PROCOMM PLUS offers very simple and systematic means of receiving, or *downloading,* a file. Since a file transfer is a cooperative effort between two different systems, you must also know how to prompt the remote system (in the case of the example below, CompuServe) to begin sending the file.

To begin this step, start PROCOMM PLUS and log onto CompuServe as you did for the preceding Step.

LOCATING A FILE

CompuServe's many forums and their libraries offer a wealth of files. If you are searching for the latest version of some shareware or public domain software, try the service called the IBM File Finder. To reach it, enter

Using the file finder

```
go ibmff
```

from a CompuServe ! prompt. For this example, we are looking for a popular file-archiving tool called PKZIP/PKUNZIP by PKWare, Inc. This set of programs shrinks files to a fraction of their original size and combines them into a single file (known as an *archive*), which can then be transmitted in a much shorter time

STEP 7

than can the original files. It then restores them to their original form. Since most of the files on bulletin boards and other services are precompressed, you will need to have a program like this on hand.

To activate the file finder from the main menu, enter **4** for Access File Finder. Since you know part of the file name, enter **6** for File Name. At the Enter File Name prompt, enter a file spec that can find any recent version of PKZIP, such as **pkz***, and the file finder will respond with a list of available copies and their locations, as shown in Figure 7.1.

The files are in the form PKZ*nnn*.EXE, where *nnn* is a three-digit version number. Look for the latest versions—in this case, PKZ 110.EXE. As line 2 in the figure shows, one current copy of the program can be found in the IBM Communications Forum, which you reach by entering

```
go ibmcom
```

at the ! prompt. (This choice is somewhat arbitrary, though it's the first current copy on the list and it uses the familiar naming convention.)

```
File Finder IBM

 1 BPROGA/Turbo Pascal v 5.x  PKZ101.EXE
 2 IBMCOM/Comm Utilities [C]  PKZ110.EXE
 3 IBMNEW/Library Tools [N]   PKZ110.EXE
 4 IBMPRO/DataCompression [P]   PKZ110.EXE
 5 IBMPRO/DataCompression [P]   PKZOS2.EXE
 6 IBMSYS/File Utilities [S]    PKZF11.ZIP
 7 IBMSYS/File Utilities [S]    PKZIP1.EXE
 8 IBMSYS/File Utilities [S]    PKZIP1.EXE
 9 IBMSYS/File Utilities [S]    PKZOS2.EXE
10 MSAPP/Other PC Apps  PKZIP1.EXE
11 MSLANG/New Uploads [L]   PKZ110.EXE
12 MSOPSYS/OS/2   PKZOS2.EXE
13 MSOPSYS/ShareWare  PKZ110.EXE
14 NOVA/Public Domain/Demo   PKZ110.EXE
15 PCVENC/PKWare   PKZ110.EXE
16 PCVENC/PKWare   PKZF11.EXE
17 WINADV/Shareware   PKZ110.EXE
18 WPSG/Hardware/DOS   PKZ110.EXE
19 XTALK/Help & Utilities   PKZ110.EXE
20 ZENITH/DOS Utilities   PKZ110.EXE

Enter choice or <CR> for more !
Alt-Z FOR HELP| ANSI    | FDX | 2400 E71 | LOG CLOSED | PRINT OFF | ON-LINE
```

- *Figure 7.1: Matching files found*

STEP 7

The remote end of the transfer

After you join this forum, follow these steps to bring up your file:

1. Enter **3** to bring up the Libraries menu.
2. Choose the appropriate library for your file. In this case, enter **2** for Comm Utilities.
3. Since you know the file name, enter **4** to download a file.
4. Enter the file name itself.

An alternative method is to enter **1** to browse through files until you find a description of the one you want. You can then narrow your search by specifying one or more descriptive keywords.

If you are not sure that you have space for the new file, browse to find it and note the approximate size in kilobytes that appears as part of its description. Most services state sizes for downloadable files somewhere. Always be sure that you have enough disk space to complete your download. PROCOMM PLUS informs you how much space is available locally, as you will read below.

5. From the Protocols menu, enter **5** for CompuServe Quick B, which is a good match for the CompuServe B protocol on PROCOMM PLUS. CompuServe B is an efficient protocol for transferring files over the CompuServe network.
6. Enter the same name,

    `pkz110.exe`

    to name the new file that you are creating.

CompuServe is unusual in prompting you for a file name to give your copy. Other services send either the existing file name or no name at all along with the file.

CompuServe signals its readiness to begin the transfer by sending a character resembling a club on a playing card (♣).

If you regularly make downloads from CompuServe, you can set PROCOMM PLUS to make a download automatically at this point on future occasions. After this transfer is over, bring up the Setup menu by pressing Alt-S. Press **t** for Terminal Options and then **g**

Receiving a File

STEP 7

The local end of the transfer

for General Options. Press **j** for item J, Enquiry (the club is the character known as ENQ, ASCII 5) and press the spacebar until the option reads "CIS B." Press Enter and then press Esc thrice to return to the terminal-mode screen. Be sure to save the new setting when prompted.

1. Press PgDn to bring up the PROCOMM PLUS Download Protocols menu.

Notice that the top line of the menu tells you how many bytes are free on the drive that you have designated for downloads. If you do not have enough space, press Esc and wait for the sender to abandon the transfer. Try the transfer again after you have created more space.

2. If CompuServe B is shown as your default protocol, just press Enter. Otherwise, press **c** to choose it.

3. If you were using a protocol such as XMODEM that does not send file names, PROCOMM PLUS would now prompt you for a name to give your new file.

4. PROCOMM PLUS now downloads the file, displaying a status window like that shown in Figure 7.2. When the

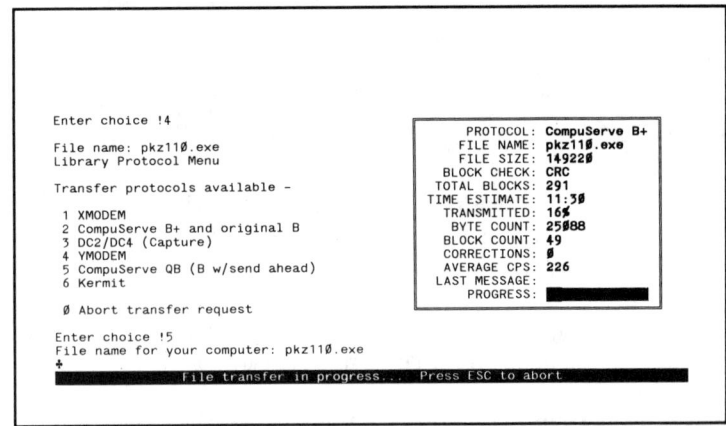

- *Figure 7.2: The downloading file-transfer window*

46 Up & Running with PROCOMM PLUS

transfer is complete, PROCOMM PLUS clears the window and sounds a bell. You can then resume working with the remote service.

Reporting of some items in the transfer-status window depends on the protocol in use. For instance, if you are using XMODEM, the window cannot report the file size or update the progress bar because PROCOMM PLUS does not know the size of the original file.

Some file-transfer protocols, such as YMODEM and ZMODEM, can transfer more than one file at a time. Using PROCOMM PLUS you can cut file names from online listings and paste them as arguments to the file-transfer command using the Screen Clip feature. See the online help (brought up by pressing first Alt-= and then Alt-Z), the User's Manual, or my book *Understanding PROCOMM PLUS* for more information.

USING THE ARCHIVING UTILITY

When you have logged off CompuServe and exited PROCOMM PLUS, take a moment to consider your new acquisition. In the context of archive files, the .EXE extension tells you that this is a *self-unpacking* archive; that is, when you execute it as a program, it disgorges its original constituent files.

It is best to unpack the archive into a new directory so that you can study its contents. Create the directory and make it current, for instance, by entering the DOS commands

```
md \pk
cd \pk
```

Enter a command consisting of your PROCOMM PLUS download path plus the base name of the archive, such as

```
c:\download\pkz110
```

substituting your path and the name of the program version that you found. The files composing the archive will be written in your

STEP 7

current directory. You should then copy the .EXE files to a directory in your DOS path. Print all files with a .DOC or .TXT extension to obtain hard copy of the documentation. You can use the DOS PRINT command for this purpose; invoke it twice in succession:

```
print *.doc
print *.txt
```

What PKZIP & PKUNZIP do

Very basically, PKZIP creates or updates archives and PKUNZIP unpacks them. The simplest command syntax for each is

```
pkzip archivename filenames...
```

to pack files described by *FILENAMES* into an archive called *ARCHIVENAME*.ZIP, or

```
pkunzip archivename
```

to unpack the files in *ARCHIVENAME*.ZIP. The archive name can include a directory path and the file names can include a path as well as wildcard characters. There are many further options, as you will read in the manual.

Registering PKWARE

PKWARE is shareware, meaning that it is distributed free with the expectation that you pay a modest charge to become a registered user if you put it to regular use. Take note of the licensing agreement and the order form included in the package; the latter tells you where to send your order. When you register, you gain advantages such as technical support and updates, and you help sustain this useful system of software distribution.

Other archiving programs

PKWARE programs work with archive files that have the extension .ZIP. For other kinds of archives, you will need other software packages. You may encounter many of these packages in the forum library that you just visited, among other sources.

Sending a File

When you send, or *upload,* a file, you follow very much the same procedure as when you receive one. First prepare the remote system for the transfer, using its own commands. Next instruct PROCOMM PLUS to carry out the upload with a few swift keystrokes. This Step shows you how to use a popular file-transfer protocol, called YMODEM. The example demonstrates an upload to a remote copy of PROCOMM PLUS that is itself running in *host mode,* which you will learn more about in Step 17.

Uploading a file in host mode with YMODEM

Although the example remote system is PROCOMM PLUS host mode, feel free to try out these techniques using an online system and files of your choice.

LOCATING YOUR FILES

You may need help recollecting the exact names or location of files that you intend to upload. As you saw in Step 4, to view the contents of a directory in PROCOMM PLUS, press Alt-F. Enter a file spec in the box that appears, or just press Enter to view all the files in a directory. PROCOMM PLUS displays matching files in a window. Figure 8.1 shows the results of entering a path name plus the file spec ***.ms** to display all files with the extension .MS in a directory. If more files match than fit in the window, the message

STEP 8

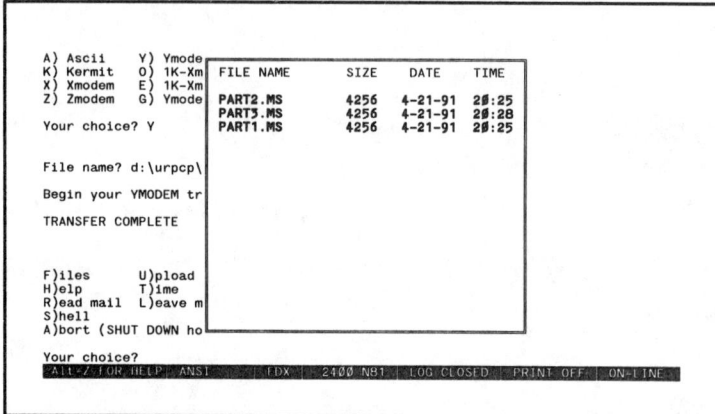

- *Figure 8.1: A file listing*

"–MORE–" will appear on the last line. You can then view another windowful of files by pressing any key. When the last windowful has been displayed, pressing any key clears the window.

You can attach a file-finder utility to PROCOMM PLUS to find a file anywhere on your system without going offline. Step 18 will show you how.

THE YMODEM PROTOCOL

This example upload uses YMODEM, an efficient protocol that can transfer a whole set of files automatically (when they have a file spec in common). This protocol is also well adapted to sending and receiving files over public networks such as the CompuServe network.

Will the real YMODEM please stand up?
The name YMODEM has been applied to more than one protocol. The protocol that appears on your PROCOMM PLUS menus as YMODEM (Batch) is widely recognized as the true YMODEM, a protocol that is capable of multiple file transfers. The protocol called YMODEM in earlier versions of PROCOMM PLUS now appears on your menus as 1K-XMODEM, in line with current practice.

50 *Up & Running with PROCOMM PLUS*

The protocols YMODEM-G (Batch) and 1K-XMODEM-G are streaming versions of YMODEM (Batch) and 1K-XMODEM, designed for use with high-speed, error-correcting modems (such as MNP or V.42 modems). Unlike the first two protocols, streaming protocols have no error-detection scheme of their own.

READYING THE REMOTE SYSTEM

For this example, log onto PROCOMM PLUS running in host mode on a second machine. Getting into host mode is more fully described in Step 17, but here are the most basic steps:

1. Start PROCOMM PLUS on the second machine and place it in host mode by pressing Alt-Q.

2. Return to the first machine and call the second, using manual dial, if you like.

3. When you are connected, give your first and last name at successive prompts. Press **y** to verify them, if they reappear correctly.

4. Enter a password of up to eight characters. Enter it again to confirm it. Press Enter to skip messages and reach the main menu, if necessary.

To prepare to upload a set of files by YMODEM, press **u** at the host mode main menu for the upload function and press **y** to pick the YMODEM protocol. At the file-name prompt, enter a file spec that covers the files you are sending. Then enter a brief description when prompted. The remote copy of PROCOMM PLUS is then prepared to receive the files.

SENDING YOUR FILES

The sequence of commands for launching an upload from PROCOMM PLUS is the same as that for a download, except that it begins by pressing PgUp instead of PgDn. The other differences in this example have to do with YMODEM and not uploads per se:

1. Press PgUp to bring up the Upload Protocols menu. In this case, there is no "bytes free" message in the window, since

Sending a File 51

STEP 8

PROCOMM PLUS has no way of knowing how much space is available on the remote system.

2. If YMODEM is shown as your default protocol, just press Enter. Otherwise, press y to choose it.

3. Enter a file spec describing the files to be uploaded. This line can also include a path name.

During the upload

PROCOMM PLUS now uploads each file in turn, while displaying a status window like that shown in Figure 8.2. Note that the window displays the name and statistics for each file as it is sent. When the last file has been transferred, the program removes the window and sounds a bell. You can then sign off the service, send a message, or do whatever else you like.

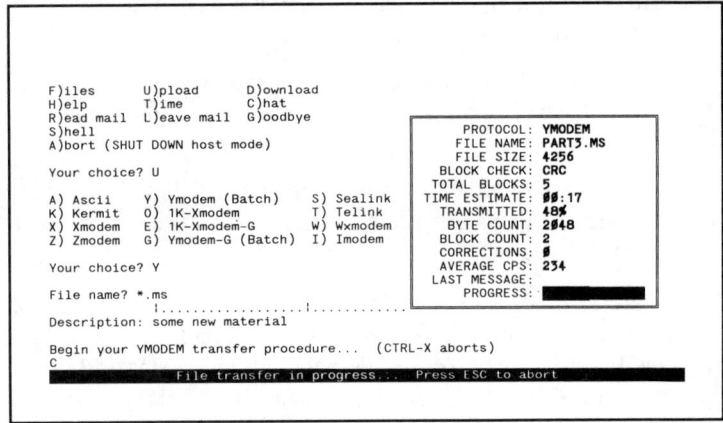

- *Figure 8.2: The uploading file-transfer window*

52 *Up & Running with PROCOMM PLUS*

Using the Editor

You will often find it convenient to call a text editor or word processor from PROCOMM PLUS to produce or edit a letter or other document. This Step acquaints you with PCEDIT, the editor provided with PROCOMM PLUS.

PCEDIT has evolved into a capable editor that can handle text files of up to 5,000 lines, at 120 columns per line. It produces ASCII text files readable by various programs and systems and takes up a modest amount of your computer's memory (about 100K). However, if you would prefer to use your own text editor or word processor in conjunction with PROCOMM PLUS, skip ahead to Step 18 to learn how to call it up while you are online. Use your editor to create a sample message like the one shown here; you will need it for Step 10.

STARTING THE EDITOR

To start PCEDIT, press Alt-A from the terminal-mode screen. PROCOMM PLUS will prompt you for a file name to supply the program. Enter **note.txt** to reach the main editing screen. Assuming that no file by this name exists, your cursor will be positioned on a blank line above a line marking the end of the file, as you can see in Figure 9.1.

STEP 9

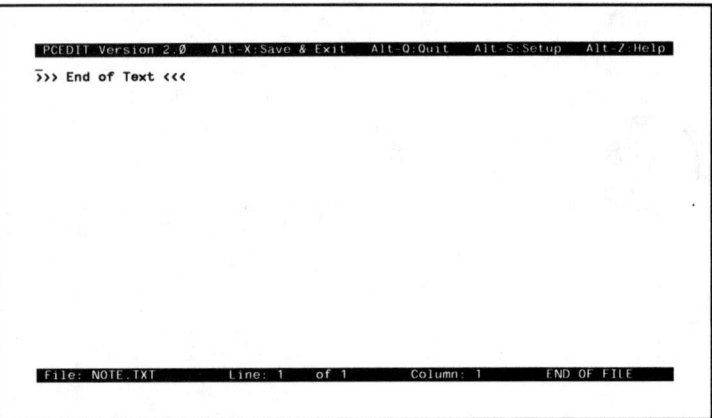

- *Figure 9.1: The PCEDIT screen*

If the program does not appear, exit PROCOMM PLUS and make sure that PCEDIT.EXE is in your PROCOMM PLUS home directory. It should have been copied there by the PCINSTAL program. If it is listed, restart PROCOMM PLUS, bring up the Setup File/Path Options screen by pressing Alt-S and then **f**, and edit option D to read "pcedit."

USING THE EDITOR

Before you begin entering text, you should make yourself aware of PCEDIT's setup and help options.

PCEDIT Setup

As with PROCOMM PLUS, bring up PCEDIT setup by pressing Alt-S from the text-entry screen. To reach the options menu for the editor, press Enter from the main menu.

To use PCEDIT for text entry, set option A—Editor input mode—to read **WP** (if it doesn't already) by pressing **a**, the spacebar, and then Enter. The WP value makes editor settings appropriate to word processing. (For instance, it enables word-wrapping at the ends of lines.) The ASPECT value makes settings useful for creating the ASPECT script files described in Steps 15 and 16.

Take a moment to note the other options in this menu. All but option E apply to WP mode. To leave the menu, press Esc.

You can set colors for various elements of the editor screen after you press c from the main menu. Step 20 describes how to set colors in PROCOMM PLUS; you can apply the instructions there directly to this PCEDIT menu. When you are done, you can return to the editor screen by pressing Esc twice and typing y to save your settings or n to leave them temporary.

PCEDIT Help

Press Alt-Z to bring up a guide that can help you use the editor. From the top, press ↓ to see available help information. It includes, successively:

- A general description of PCEDIT.
- A description of command-line options that you can use when you call PCEDIT from DOS or when you are prompted for parameters after you press Alt-A.
- A table of keystrokes that you can use while editing. Note that the Ins key controls whether you are inserting text or overwriting previous text. The cursor is made taller in overwrite mode.
- A further table of Alt-key and Ctrl-key combination keystrokes.
- A table of keystroke macros to simplify entry of ASPECT scripts.

Press Esc now to return to the entry screen.

Entering a Note

Begin by typing in a date, pressing Enter a couple of times, and typing in

    Dear Your Name,

using your own name (you will send this message to yourself).

STEP 9

Now instead of pressing Enter, press Alt-P to leave a blank line and move the cursor to the paragraph indent. Type in a couple of lines of text, such as:

```
Thank you for your recent communication. I am
glad to hear that the project is going well
and look forward to hearing more about it.
```

Allow PCEDIT to wrap words over successive lines.

When you start PCEDIT, it is ready to overwrite existing text. Switch to insert mode by pressing Ins. Use the arrow keys to move the cursor to any point within the first line of your text and add some words; note that PCEDIT continues to wrap words over the following lines. Delete the new phrase; this time word-wrapping does not take effect. You can reformat your paragraph, however, by pressing Ctrl-F.

Moving through the File

As you typed, previous lines scrolled off the top of the screen. Press Ctrl-PgUp to go to the top of the file; this makes the whole note visible. Try some of the cursor-movement keys listed in the help screens. In particular, note that the Home or End key places you, respectively, at the first or beyond the last character in a given line (not counting spaces).

Searching for Text

In such a short file, searches and block operations are hardly needed, but try these examples to see the technique.

Press Ctrl-PgUp to return to the top of the file. (Searches begin at the cursor position.) Press Alt-F to find text and enter a word that occurs in the text, such as "**project**." Note that it doesn't matter whether your search string or the text is upper- or lowercase. PCEDIT will place the first line containing the text at the top of the screen, highlight the search term, and place the cursor under the first character. You can look for subsequent lines containing

56   *Up & Running with PROCOMM PLUS*

the word (but not subsequent occurrences in the same line) by pressing Alt-N.

Working with Blocks of Text

Block operations in PCEDIT always use whole lines of text. For instance, to mark the line that reads "Dear *Your Name*," move the cursor into any position on that line and press Alt-B. You can expand the marked area by pressing ↑ and ↓. Press ↑ once now to include the blank line above in the marked area, then press Alt-B again to end marking. At this point, you can perform a number of operations on the block using Alt-key combinations listed in the help screens. For instance, you can:

- Press Alt-E to erase the marked block
- Move the cursor to a line and press Alt-C to make a copy of the block below the cursor line
- Move the cursor to a line and press Alt-M to move the block below the cursor line

Try copying the block to below the last line, then try remarking and deleting the new lines.

LEAVING THE EDITOR

As noted on the top line of the screen, you can save your changes and leave PCEDIT by pressing Alt-X, or you can discard your changes and exit by pressing Alt-Q and then pressing Enter to confirm your intentions. Press Alt-X now to save your sample file.

Making ASCII File Transfers

This Step gives you a chance to upload and download a file via an ASCII file transfer.

ASCII transfers are not as sophisticated as transfers that use full-fledged file-transfer protocols, which provide for error detection. In fact, ASCII transfers consist of a simple stream of text characters—just like your keyboard input, except much faster. However, they are sometimes the only means available for transferring text files.

A simple transfer procedure

One very common application for ASCII transfers allows you to upload a precomposed file to a system that is expecting you to compose, say, an electronic mail message online. Writing the message ahead of time and uploading it can save you expensive connect time, permitting you the luxury of careful writing and editing.

You need not transfer a file using an ASCII transfer just because it is a text file—a regular file-transfer protocol may be more reliable and error-free.

CONDUCTING AN ASCII UPLOAD

For this exercise, you can gain experience with ASCII transfers by uploading your message of the previous Step to your CompuServe

STEP 10

account and then downloading it. To begin, log onto CompuServe and position yourself at any ! prompt. Bring up the electronic mail service by entering

```
go mail
```

Preparing the Remote System

The first step in an upload is to prepare the remote system to accept input as data to be placed into a file. From the CompuServe Mail main menu, enter **3** to upload a message. Then enter **4** for "NO protocol"—this is equivalent to an ASCII transfer. Enter **n** at the prompt,

```
Do you want to be prompted for each line (Y or
N)?
```

because you want to make one continuous upload. CompuServe responds with this message:

```
Begin sending your data. Use /EX to indicate
the end of your data.
```

CompuServe will now begin placing the characters you send into a temporary storage area. Note that a system always accepts a special key sequence to indicate the end of input. For CompuServe Mail, it is the characters "/ex." Elsewhere, it might be Ctrl-D, pressing Enter twice, or something else.

Preparing PROCOMM PLUS

Press PgUp as you did for a CompuServe B or YMODEM upload. From the Upload Protocols menu, enter **a** to choose ASCII. Enter the name for your file, **note.txt**, as shown in Figure 10.1.

Making the Upload

As you press Enter, PROCOMM PLUS begins sending the file. When it has finished (i.e., the bell sounds and the transfer message

```
1 XMODEM (MODEM7) protocol
2 CompuServe 'B' protocol
3 DC2/DC4 CAPTURE protocol
4 NO Protocol
5 Kermit
6 CompuServe Quick 'B' protocol

        ─┤ ASCII UPLOAD ├─
         Please enter filename: note.txt_
Enter

No error detection/correction.
Do you want to be prompted for each line (Y or N)? n

Begin sending your data. Use
/EX to indicate the end of your
data.

Alt-Z FOR HELP| ANSI    | FDX |  2400 E71 | LOG CLOSED | PRINT OFF | ON-LINE
```

- *Figure 10.1: Sending a file via ASCII*

is cleared from the status line), enter /ex on a line by itself to signal the end of the transfer to CompuServe.

The file contents and your keyboard input are indistinguishable to the remote system. If you like, you can put the "end of input" characters at the end of files that you send. For instance, you could have made "/ex" the last line of NOTE.TXT.

Mailing the Message

A few more steps are necessary to actually put your uploaded message into the mail. Press Enter at the CompuServe "Press <CR>:" prompt. Enter **1** to send the message at the following menu. At successive prompts, enter your own user ID number, the subject **Test Message**, and your name. CompuServe will repeat this information to allow you to confirm it. Enter **y** if everything is correct.

Enter **bye** at the main-menu prompt and press Alt-H to hang up at the "Host Name:" prompt. Sit back and allow a few minutes for your mail to reach you. Log onto CompuServe again and look for the message

Getting your mail

```
You have Electronic Mail waiting
```

Making ASCII File Transfers 61

If you don't see this message, log off again and wait a little longer. When you do see it, return to CompuServe mail by entering **go mail** as before.

CONDUCTING AN ASCII DOWNLOAD

An ASCII download is the opposite of an ASCII upload. Here you prepare PROCOMM PLUS to place incoming text into a file and then give the remote system the go-ahead to send the text.

Setting Up the Transfer

Enter **1** at the Mail main menu to read the message. After it scrolls by, you will see a menu for disposition of the message. Enter **7** to dowload the message. As before, enter **4** to signify "NO Protocol." When CompuServe sends the prompt

```
Key <CR> when ready:
```

it is ready to send the file. (Note that CompuServe does not word its prompts consistently.)

Preparing PROCOMM PLUS

Press PgDn and enter **a** to choose an ASCII download. Enter **note2.txt** as a new file name for your downloaded file. You can precede the name with a path; if you do not, PROCOMM PLUS will create the file in your default download directory.

Making the Download

With the file window cleared, press Enter. PROCOMM PLUS forwards your keystroke to CompuServe, which takes it as a signal to send the file. After the file is sent, CompuServe sends the prompt

```
Press <CR>!
```

At this point, press Esc to tell PROCOMM PLUS that the transfer is complete. Then press Enter to bring up the next CompuServe menu. You can now enter **1** to delete the message from the CompuServe system. Log off the system by entering **bye** and pressing Alt-H as before.

THE NEW FILE

The newly received file, as displayed by PCEDIT, is shown in Figure 10.2. Note that additional starting and ending prompts are inevitably grafted onto ASCII transfers, but you can edit them out. The prompts show the control-character sequences that CompuServe uses to write to ANSI terminals. (They begin with ←[.)

ASCII TRANSFER OPTIONS

Before exiting PROCOMM PLUS, bring up the ASCII Protocol Options menu by pressing Alt-S, and then **p** and **a**. This menu controls details of ASCII transfers. Here are some options to consider:

- **Echo locally:** if you set this option to YES, you will be able to see an upload in progress, even if the remote system does not echo (retransmit) what you are sending.

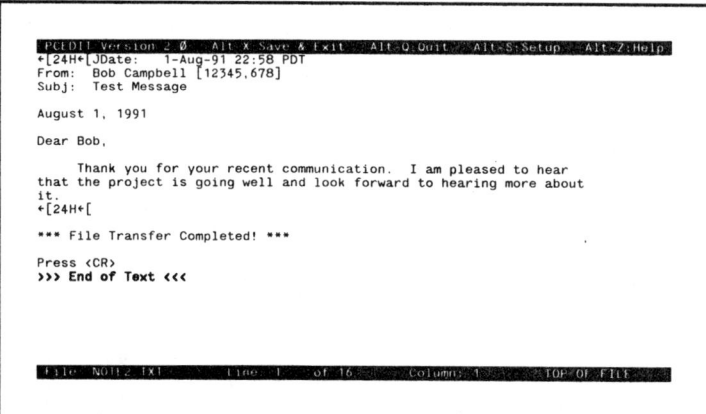

- *Figure 10.2: The new file*

STEP 10

- **Expand blank lines:** this means inserting spaces between pairs of line endings (so that you can send files with blank lines to systems that use two successive carriage returns to signal the end of input).

- **Character pacing and line pacing:** these options allow you to add pauses between individual characters and whole lines to accommodate slow systems, which may not be prepared to accept input much faster than ordinary typing.

- **CR translation and LF translation:** these options alter line endings to allow you to match your files to the expectations of remote systems. For instance, you can set carriage-return translation (upload) to NONE and line-feed translation (upload) to STRIP to make your uploaded text file look more like keyboard input, in which lines end with carriage returns only.

These options are briefly described in the help screen that appears if you press Alt-Z at this point.

Return from this help screen to the terminal-mode screen by pressing Esc three times; then exit the program.

Using External Protocols

PROCOMM PLUS allows you to call an external program to extend its file-transfer capabilities. This Step offers you a chance to try this technique by making a download.

The program used for this Step, called DSZ, offers a more advanced version of the ZMODEM file-transfer protocol than PROCOMM PLUS itself incorporates. It also includes its own implementations of the XMODEM, XMODEM-1K, and YMODEM protocols. You can download ZMODEM from CompuServe. Use the IBM File Finder to find DSZ.ZIP, just as you found PKZIP.EXE for Step 7. DSZ is also found on many bulletin boards.

Using a more sophisticated protocol

When you have DSZ.ZIP, unpack its contents. Copy the files with the .COM, .EXE, and .BAT extensions to a directory on your path. If you are using a serial port other than COM1, to allow DSZ to find it, create a new environment variable by entering

```
set dszport=n
```

where *n* is your serial port.

STEP 11

SETTING UP THE PROTOCOL

Follow these steps to set up DSZ as an external protocol:

1. Press Alt-S, **p**, and then **e** to bring up the Setup External Protocol Options menu.

2. Select Option A (Name) and enter **DSZ** as the name of the first external protocol, as it will appear on PROCOMM PLUS windows and menus.

3. Leave Option B (Type set to PROGRAM) to call an ordinary program such as DSZ.

4. Select Option C (Upload command) and enter **dsz sz** (send ZMODEM) to call DSZ and pass it a parameter that tells it to make a ZMODEM upload.

5. Select Option D (Download command) and enter **dsz rz** (receive ZMODEM) to invoke the program for a ZMODEM download. Downloads will be made to your current directory. If, however, you obtain a registered copy of ZMODEM, you can add your default download path to this field as a further parameter.

6. Press Esc and type **z** for the ZMODEM options menu. If option C (Auto downloading) is set to ON, change the setting to OFF. (If the setting were left ON, PROCOMM PLUS would start its own ZMODEM download automatically before you could call the external protocol.)

7. Return to the terminal-mode screen and save your changes by pressing Esc three times and then pressing **y**.

CONTACTING A SERVICE

Choosing the LIST utility

You must find an online service that uses ZMODEM to try out this technique. If you are willing to make a call to Northern California, you can take this opportunity to download the latest version of LIST—an invaluable file-browse utility—from the bulletin board

STEP 11

maintained by its author. Bring up the dialing directory by pressing Alt-D from the terminal-mode screen and make a new entry using these values:

```
        NAME:  VOR BBS
      NUMBER:  1 (707) 778-8944
        BAUD:  2400 [or whatever is applicable]
      PARITY:  NONE
   DATA BITS:  8
   STOP BITS:  1
       DUPLEX: FULL
        PORT:  DEFAULT [or whatever you use]
      SCRIPT:
    PROTOCOL:  DSZ
    TERMINAL:  ANSI
        MODE:  MODEM
```

You can leave the SCRIPT field blank. Press Enter to dial the new entry. Follow the prompts carefully when you first sign on to any bulletin board. You will be asked, as a minimum, to give a first name, a last name, and a password. Make up a password, but be sure to note it for future logins. If you have a color monitor, you can choose to display graphics or not; graphics make menus more colorful and readable but slow their display.

Bulletin boards provide varied means for picking a file-transfer protocol. On the example board, when you reach the main menu, choose a default protocol by entering **t** for Transfer Protocol, then **z** for ZMODEM.

Next, from the main menu, enter **f** for Files, press Enter again, and then enter **1** for the first file directory—the Buerg utilities. Scroll through these pages of entries until you see an entry in the form LIST*nnn*.ZIP (or .ARC, or .EXE), where *nnn* is a version number. Stop viewing the listings by entering **n** at the bottom of the screen.

Using External Protocols

STEP 11

Choosing files to download

MAKING THE DOWNLOAD

At this point, enter **d** for download. ZMODEM allows batch transfers, and this board exploits this fact by allowing you to name two or more successive files to download. Enter the name of the file(s) you found, then press Enter to signify no more files. The bulletin board will show you some useful statistics and prompt you for some further choices, as shown in Figure 11.1. Press Enter to begin the transfer and remain logged on after it is over.

Press PgDn to begin the download at your end. Notice that item 1, DSZ, has become the default choice for this entry. Press Enter to choose it. Press Enter at the Parameters window, since no additional parameters need be passed.

PROCOMM PLUS will call the external protocol, which actually undertakes the local end of the transfer, as shown in Figure 11.2. When DSZ terminates, you will be returned to the PROCOMM PLUS terminal-mode screen. At this point, you can log off the bulletin board by pressing Enter twice, then **g** for goodbye at the main menu.

```
                                    printer with headings, pagination, etc. w/ASM
        LP16.ARC        9611  06-19-86  Print a file on HP laserjet with heading and
                                    settable cpi/lpi. V.Buerg, w/ASM
        LUBUERG.LBR    26752  05-08-86  COM and DQC for LUD/LUE/LUT/LUU
        LUD106.LBR      3584  07-08-85  D)elete and R)eorg functions of LU
        LUE220.COM      2988  04-28-86  Extract and expand LBR files
        LUE220.DOC      4813  04-28-86  Documentation for LUE 2.10
        LUE220.LBR      6272  04-28-86  Extract and unsqueeze LBR file members.
        LUT193.LBR      3712  05-28-85  Display LBR directories

        (H)elp, (1-30), File List Command? d

        (1) Enter the filename to Download (Enter)=none? list75g.arc
        Checking file transfer request. Please wait, Bob ...
        (1)     LIST75G.ARC  119814 bytes,  9 minutes (approximate) FREE / NO TIME

        (2) Enter the filename to Download (Enter)=none?

        Batch Download Time:   9 minutes (approximate)
        Batch Download Size:   119814 bytes (118 blocks)
        Batch Protocol Type:   Zmodem        (Batch U/L and D/L)
        (Ready to Send in Batch Mode)

        (G)oodbye after Batch, (A)bort or (E)dit Batch, (Enter)=continue? ( )
        Alt-Z FOR HELP| ANSI   | FDX  | 2400 N81 | LOG CLOSED | PRINT OFF | ON-LINE
```

- *Figure 11.1: Commands to the remote service*

```
DSZ (TurboC) Copyright 02-28-91 by Omen Technology INC
         "The High Reliability Software"

Registration and Documentation: $20 Check/MO
Omen Technology Inc, P.O. BOX 4681, Portland OR 97208

VISA/MC ZERO PAPERWORK Registration!  Data: 503-621-3746
VOICE: 503-621-3406

COM2 2400 bps   Carrier Detect enabled  Handshake both S/N 0
Command line = 'rz '
list75g.arc       937 sectors 119814 bytes Estimated   9.2 Min
   7168 ZMODEM CRC-32   _
```

- *Figure 11.2: DSZ in action*

BROWSING THROUGH THE DOWNLOADED FILE

To try the LIST file-browse utility, exit the program, create and move to a new directory, and unpack the archive contents into this directory as you did for PKZIP in Step 7. Print the document file LIST.DOC and move LIST.COM into a directory on your path. You can then study the documentation and try out various commands.

Using the LIST utility

LIST is not public-domain software but must be licensed for corporate use. Note also that DSZ, downloaded earlier in this Step, is shareware that you should register. Registration or licensing instructions are among the document files in both the DSZ and LIST packages.

Registration and licensing

Using External Protocols

STEP 12

Using Kermit

Kermit is a highly adaptable file-transfer protocol that can make transfers between many kinds of systems over varied conditions. In this final Step on file transfers, you will have a chance to try out its two usual modes of operation, *interactive mode* and *server mode*.

The remote system in the example is Berkeley UNIX. In the past, to gain access to a UNIX system, you had to obtain an account at a university or other institution. Recently, public online UNIX systems based on PCs with 80386 processors are becoming more common. You may find a few such systems listed in your local computer journal.

Accessing a remote system

Start PROCOMM PLUS, dial your system, and follow the directions you have been given to log on. For a typical institutional system, you enter successively a UNIX system name, your special logon ID, and your password. Then you normally press Enter to verify that your terminal type corresponds to the one that the remote system expects. This should bring you to the UNIX command prompt.

Logging on to the system

STEP 12

STARTING KERMIT

On the example system, enter **kermit** to start the remote Kermit program, then enter any commands necessary to adapt Kermit to your local conditions. Two such commands are necessary for the example setup. The first,

    set parity even

changes the parity on the system from none to even. This is necessary because the line to the remote system has even parity, although the remote Kermit defaults to no parity (you could learn this by giving the remote Kermit the **show** command and noting the parity setting). The second command,

    set file type text

optimizes the system for text-file transmission.

This last point bears further discussion. When Kermit is set to send a text file, it translates the original file into a standard text-file format on the destination machine. When it is set to send a binary file (such as a program, an archive, or a bitmapped graphics file), it makes no such translations. The Kermits at both ends of the line must therefore agree on the file type.

To set Kermit to transfer text files, press Alt-S and then **k** to bring up the Kermit Options menu. If item H (File type) is not set to TEXT, press **h**, the spacebar, and then Enter to change it. Return to the terminal-mode screen as usual. This is the only use that you must make of this menu in most cases.

UPLOADING A FILE

At this point, to upload a file, enter **receive**.

Figure 12.1 shows the commands to the remote Kermit and its responses up to this point in the example. Press PgUp, type **k** for Kermit, and enter the name of the file to send. Because Kermit handles batch-file transfers, you can use a file spec with wildcard characters to send a whole set of files. PROCOMM PLUS then displays the Kermit transfer window shown in Figure 12.2. Kermit will translate the file names according to the conventions of the target system, if necessary. When the transfer is completed, you are returned to the prompt of the remote Kermit. Exit Kermit and return to the UNIX prompt by entering the command **exit**.

```
% kermit
C-Kermit, 4E(072) 24 Jan 89, 4.2 BSD
Type ? for help
C-Kermit>set parity even
C-Kermit>set file type text
C-Kermit>receive
Escape back to your local system and give a SEND command...
_




                                                                        

 Alt-Z FOR HELP| VT102    | FDX |  2400 E71 | LOG OPEN   | PRINT OFF | ON-LINE
```

- *Figure 12.1: Starting a Kermit upload*

```
% kermit
C-Kermit, 4E(072) 24 Jan 89, 4.2 BSD
Type ? for help
C-Kermit>set parity even
C-Kermit>set file
C-Kermit>receive          PROTOCOL: Kermit
Escape back to yo        FILE NAME: STEP11.MS
                         FILE SIZE: 4972
                         FILE TYPE: TEXT
                       FILE NUMBER: 1
                       COMPRESSION: YES
                      8 BIT PREFIX: YES
                       WINDOW SIZE: 0
                       BLOCK CHECK: 1 BYTE CHECKSUM
                     TRANSFER TIME: 00:26 (Approximate)
                        BYTE COUNT: 242
                      LAST MESSAGE: File header transferred



      ESC: Abort Transfer    CTRL-B: Cancel Batch    CTRL-F: Cancel File
```

- *Figure 12.2: An upload in progress*

STEP 12

Using Kermit

STEP 12

DOWNLOADING A FILE

To inaugurate a download from a remote Kermit, follow the same steps as for an upload except that, after you set up the remote Kermit, give it the command

    send filespec

where *filespec* covers the set of files that you want. At this point, press PgDn and type **k** to tell PROCOMM PLUS that you are making a Kermit download. The Kermit transfer window then appears (you need not specify file names, because they will be sent along with the files themselves). As with a Kermit upload, you are returned to the remote Kermit's prompt when the transfer is complete.

Be mindful that file-naming conventions vary from system to system. For instance, UNIX file names, unlike DOS file names, may have more than three characters in their extensions, and they may at times be distinguished by their case alone: sample.txt, Sample.txt, and SAMPLE.TXT are three different files to UNIX. Kermit will rename files to avoid name collisions on the target system.

USING THE SERVER MODE

A quick way to transfer files

Server mode is a Kermit function that can simplify routine file transfers. Here you first set up the remote Kermit as a server and then bring up a special PROCOMM PLUS menu with a restricted range of commands. You then communicate with the remote Kermit indirectly, through this menu.

If need be, you can restart the remote Kermit, giving it the same initialization commands as for uploads and downloads. After that, all you need do is enter the command **server**.

Choosing the server functions

When the remote Kermit is ready, press Alt-K to bring up the PROCOMM PLUS menu shown in Figure 12.3. Press the number

74 *Up & Running with PROCOMM PLUS*

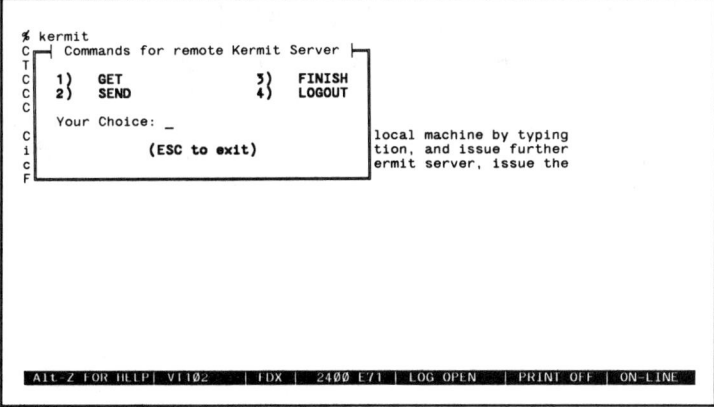

- *Figure 12.3: The Server menu*

corresponding to the function you want performed:

- **1** to GET (download) a file or files—you will be prompted for a file spec; when you enter it, the download will proceed
- **2** to SEND (upload) a file or files—you will be prompted as above
- **3** to FINISH server mode and return to the remote Kermit's prompt
- **4** to LOGOUT and exit Kermit; in most cases, this logs you off the remote system as well

After you have completed a file transfer, press Alt-K again to choose another server operation.

After you have chosen FINISH, you should terminate the remote Kermit by entering **exit** and log off the remote UNIX system by entering **logout** for Berkeley UNIX systems—or pressing Ctrl-D for System V UNIX—at the system prompt. You can then hang up and exit PROCOMM PLUS as usual.

Logging off Kermit

STEP 12

LEARNING MORE ABOUT KERMIT

Kermit has many refinements and variations that may or may not be implemented on a given remote system. Read *Kermit, a File Transfer Protocol* (by Frank da Cruz, Digital Press, 1987) to learn more about this protocol, and my *Understanding PROCOMM PLUS* for more details on the use of Kermit with PROCOMM PLUS.

Record Keeping

This Step brings together the functions that PROCOMM PLUS offers you to record, document, and keep track of an online session. With them, you can record how long you've been connected, review material that has just scrolled past on the screen and save it, record the current screen contents, and record your session as it progresses. PROCOMM PLUS also keeps its own log of services that you've contacted, together with the dates and times that you were connected.

Keeping track of your online session

To try out these features, start PROCOMM PLUS and log onto CompuServe as you have for previous Steps.

SEEING THE ELAPSED TIME

After you have been connected for a moment, press Alt-T to display a window showing the current date and time, as well as the elapsed time since you began the connection (Figure 13.1). Press any key to clear the display.

THE REDISPLAY BUFFER

As material scrolls off screen, it is not immediately lost; the most recent part of your session is still available in the *redisplay buffer*,

STEP 13

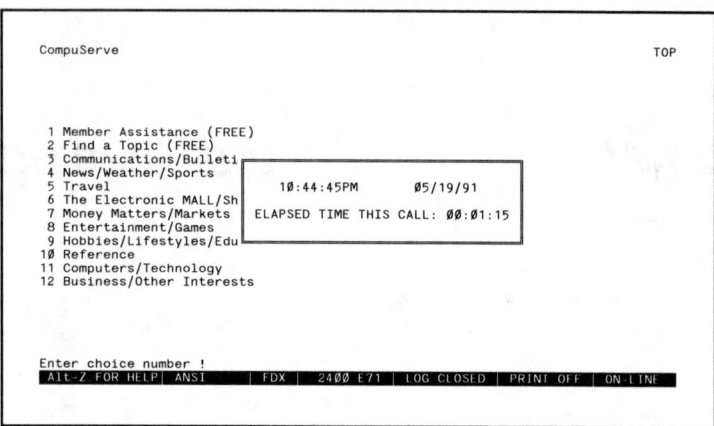

- *Figure 13.1: The elapsed time display*

which you can view with a keystroke. You can also copy the contents of this buffer to a file.

Sizing the redisplay buffer

One nice feature is that you can choose how much previous material to save: Press Alt-S and then **d** from the terminal-mode screen to bring up the Setup Display/Sound Options menu. Then select option H and enter the number of kilobytes to save. Note that a larger buffer requires more computer memory.

To suspend the scrolling on CompuServe and many other systems, press Ctrl-S. When you have finished reading, press Ctrl-Q to signal the remote system to resume sending material.

Suppose that you are joining a CompuServe forum and realize that the introductory material is worth reading, only to see it scroll off the screen before you can read it. Simulate this situation now by signing onto the Graphics Support Forum (a source for computer graphics and animation materials) by entering

```
go graphsupport
```

at the ! prompt. (Find another new forum if you are already a member of this one.) Notice that more than one screenful of text scrolls past before you are first invited to press Enter. When you

78 *Up & Running with PROCOMM PLUS*

reach the main forum menu, press Alt-F6 to activate the redisplay. Note the choices shown on the status line: you can position yourself in the buffer by pressing ↑, ↓, PgUp, PgDn, Home, or End. As explained below, you can press **f** to find text or **w** to write the entire buffer out to a file. By pressing Esc, you return to the terminal-mode screen. Use the positioning keys to place the beginning of the welcoming text at the top of the screen, as shown in Figure 13.2.

Finding Text

To find a word that you happened to catch scrolling by, press **f** for Find. Enter (for instance) **member** at the prompt in the status line. The first instance of this text in the buffer is highlighted. To find further instances of the same text, you need only press **f** and then Enter. The search matches both upper- and lowercase versions of your text and proceeds from the current top line of the screen down to the end of the buffer.

Saving the Buffer

To save the buffer to a file, press **w** for Write and enter a file name such as "graph.spt" at the prompt in the status line. The contents

```
Welcome to The Graphics Support Forum.

The Graphics Support Forum is dedicated to the support of online graphics. Our
libraries contain programs and utilities that will assist our members in their
endeavors in regards to viewing graphics online or downloading them for offline
viewing.

We know that you are not a member of the forum yet, and we hope that you will
take the time to join us and take part in our forum activities. It will cost
you nothing extra to join, beyond normal CompuServe connect and communications
surcharges.

To join, select Option 8 from the Main Menu, or type JOIN, at any forum prompt.
Please use your full name when joining; 'handles' are not encouraged.

The world of online computer graphics is one of the newest and most interesting
areas of the computer industry today, and GIF (pronounced "JIF") images are
designed to satisfy a wide variety of graphics requirements.

GIF images can be created and viewed with nearly any type of computer system,
making them ideal for the exchange of images among users of differing hardware.
Our libraries are filled with thousands of these colorful and imaginative GIF

Press <CR> for more :
↑/↓/PgUp/PgDn/Home/End:Movement keys  C:Clipboard  F:Find  W:Write  ESC:Exit
```

- *Figure 13.2: Redisplaying the opening screen*

STEP 13

will be copied to a text file in the current directory for your later reference. You can also specify a path name for the file.

Printing the Buffer

If you must, you can print the buffer's contents immediately by entering the DOS-reserved name for your printer (for instance, "prn" or "lpt2") as a file name. This is not recommended, however, since printing is time consuming, and your session may be disrupted if you have a printer problem.

When you are done, return to the terminal-mode screen by pressing Esc. Join the forum by entering first **8** and then your name.

TAKING A SCREEN SNAPSHOT

Sometimes you may want to save only the current screen. To save the forum menu that you are now viewing, press Alt-G. The word "SNAPSHOT" appears briefly on the status line as the screen contents are saved to a text file called PCPLUS.SCR in the current directory.

If PCPLUS.SCR already exists, the new screen contents are appended to it.

LOGGING YOUR FILES

Besides being an invaluable way to keep a record of a session (as you saw in Step 6), the file-logging feature is handy for capturing more than a screenful of quickly scrolling information. You can later review the material offline with your file browser or editor, avoiding stress and saving connect-time charges in the process.

Finding the catalog

For instance, forum library sections include a text catalog of files in that section. This catalog is quicker to peruse than the descriptions offered by the BROWSE choice at the section menu, but more informative than the DIRECTORY choice. To capture this file from one of the Graphics Support forum sections, enter **3** for

LIBRARIES from the main menu, and then enter **9** for Graphics Demos. Enter **1** to browse the listings and enter the keywords **text catalog**. Press Enter to skip the prompt for dates. At the catalog listing, enter **choices**.

Your next command to CompuServe will cause the catalog to scroll by. To capture it, first press Alt-F1 and enter the name **demos** for the log file. Then enter **1** for "READ this file" at the CompuServe prompt. Figure 13.3 shows these catalog listings at the point of filling the screen and scrolling off it. When you see the "Press <CR> !" prompt signifying that the whole listing has been shown to you, first press Alt-F1 to turn off the file-logging feature, then press Enter to continue to the next listing. You can return to the Demos menu by pressing **m**. You can then log off CompuServe by entering **bye** as usual.

Capturing the catalog

Pausing Logging to a File

Note that you can pause logging to a file at any point by pressing Alt-F2. The message "LOG ON HOLD" will appear on the status line. Like Alt-F1, this key is a toggle; pressing it a second time causes logging to resume. You can use this sequence to exclude a block of the catalog (or other material) from your log.

```
Graphics Support Forum (GO PICS)
LIB 12:  Graphics Demos I
One-line Descriptions of all files as of Tuesday April 30, 1991

Name/Type        Size  Date       Description
---------        ----  ---------  -----------
123DEM.EXE  B    433K  22-Dec-90  Lotus 123 Release 3 Demo with lots of animation
1988EG.ZIP  B    195K  05-Apr-90  Asteroid Collision
3.EXE       B    233K  02-Apr-90  Netherlands Foreign Investment Agency InterAd
3DEYE.ZIP   B     63K  09-Sep-90  3D FLI Animation of an eye tumbling over a sphere
AAPLAY.ZIP  B     55K  04-Jan-90  Player/Viewer for Autodesk Animator .FLI files
ADOBIL.ZIP  B    107K  05-Mar-90  Review of Adobe Illustrator
APPLAU.ZIP  B    703K  06-Mar-90  Animated demo of Aston Tate's "Applause"
AVMSHO.EXE  B    113K  02-Feb-90  Animation describing a slide service
BOUNCE.ZIP  B    473K  27-Mar-91  BOUNCE.ZIP - 3D raytraced animation
CCPDEM.EXE  B    402K  22-Dec-90  Intel Connection Co-Processor Demo good animation
CONE.ZIP    B     21K  26-Apr-90  Cone into Sphere
CUBIST.ZIP  B    305K  07-Sep-90  Cubist.zip - Raytraced 3D Animation of A Jade Scul
CYCLE.ZIP   B     11K  12-Jun-90  Cycle.zip
D2SNDS.EXE  B     55K  26-Jun-90  Demo2 Sound Effect Program by Silver Tongue SW
DAZZLE.ZIP  B     65K  11-Dec-90  Dazzle 4.0 VGA Kaleidoscope Program for IBM's
DIST.ZIP    B    149K  03-Jun-90  Dust in the Wind
DRAPPL.ZIP  B     42K  05-Mar-90  Review of Ashton Tate's "Applause"
EGACRD.ZIP  B    381K  19-Dec-9
Alt-Z FOR HELP| ANSI   | FDX | 2400 E71 | LOG OPEN | PRINT OFF | ON-LINE
```

■ *Figure 13.3: A library catalog*

STEP 13

Printing Online

You can start an instantaneously printed transcript of your session by pressing Alt-L, with your printer turned on and connected to PRN (or the device specified as Setup General Option A). Material will be printed until you press Alt-L a second time. While you are printing, the message "PRINT ON" appears in the status line.

Because printing greatly slows your online activity, and because your session could be disrupted by printer problems such as running out of paper, it is recommended that you log material to a file for later printing as described above, instead of printing it immediately.

LOGGING YOUR CALLS

Using the built-in log

PROCOMM PLUS keeps its own record of your calls in a log file named PCPLUS.FON, maintained in the PCPLUS home directory. Try viewing this log using PROCOMM PLUS's built-in viewer, which you can call up from the terminal-mode screen by pressing Alt-V and entering a path name and file name. The keystrokes available to you are shown on the viewer's status line.

As you see, each line is a record of a call completed, with the name and number from a dialing-directory entry, as well as the date, starting time, ending time, and elapsed time of the connection.

You can prevent PROCOMM PLUS from maintaining a call log, if you like, by turning off item H, Call Logging, in the Setup General Options menu (first press Alt-S and then type **g**).

STEP 14

Using Meta Keys

PROCOMM PLUS makes a set of ten key combinations available for you to define and use as you will. You can define any of these combinations to send a series of keystrokes to a remote system (thus making it a keyboard macro), invoke an external program, or execute a script to automate a series of operations. This Step treats Meta keys as keyboard macros; you will learn more about executing scripts in Steps 15 and 16, and running external programs in Step 18.

What's a Meta key?

A *keyboard macro* is a means of reducing a sequence of commonly used keystrokes to a single key combination, which saves effort and is easier to recall. With PROCOMM PLUS, each of your macros can replace up to 50 individual keystrokes. A macro can include all the characters you send to a remote system, among them regular printing characters and control characters such as carriage returns, tabs, and backspaces. It can also include a special character used to create a half-second pause between other characters.

What's a keyboard macro?

In this Step, you will define some helpful keyboard macros for use with your CompuServe account.

STEP 14

CREATING A MACRO

From the terminal-mode screen, bring up the Meta-key window by pressing Alt-M. Note that Meta keys may be assigned to Alt-1 through Alt-0. The bottom line shows keystrokes now available and their corresponding actions, as explained below.

For instance, to assign a key sequence to Alt-1, highlight its line with ↑ or ↓, press Tab to accept the TEXT Meta key type (which applies to keyboard macros), and press **r** for Revise. The cursor will be moved to a highlighted area following the key name. Use the normal editing keys shown on the inside back cover to edit the entry.

Enter your nine-character CompuServe user ID here. The macro should simulate your pressing Enter to send your ID. To do this, add the two characters ^m to the end of the entry. These translate into the ASCII control character Ctrl-M, which is synonymous with a carriage return or press of the Enter key. Press Enter to complete the entry of the new macro definition.

You can make a similar entry for your password, but note that once you save this set of macros, the file that they are kept in—as well as this window itself—will be available to anyone who uses your computer.

CREATING A PAUSE

Often after you have entered a command on CompuServe, you must wait while the system shifts from area to area before you can enter another command. You can simulate a wait like this by adding pause characters to a macro definition.

Highlight the Alt-2 line, type **r**, press Tab, and enter the following definition:

    go ibmff^m~~~~~~4^m

This sequence will take you to the IBM File Finder, wait three seconds for it to appear, and make the menu choice to access the finder. Each tilde character adds ½ second to the total pause.

Once you have entered the two definitions above, your macro window should resemble the one shown in Figure 14.1. Try creating one or two additional macros to automate your most frequent commands to CompuServe.

If you need the tilde character for its literal significance, you can choose another character to represent a pause. After you remove the keyboard macro window as described below, bring up the Setup General Options menu by pressing Alt-S and **g** from the terminal-mode screen. Press **f** and enter the character of your choice. Return to the terminal-mode screen, saving your setting as usual.

Redefining the tilde

A shortcoming of the pause character is that if the remote system is bogged down, your pause may not be long enough; the system may not yet be ready for further input. It would be helpful if PROCOMM PLUS could wait for a specific prompt before sending a command instead of pausing a fixed time. You can enable the program to do just that, using the script files illustrated in Steps 15 and 16.

```
META KEYS: PCPLUS.KEY

         TYPE   CONTENTS
Alt-1    TEXT   12345,678^m
Alt-2    TEXT   go ibmff^m~~~~~4^m
Alt-3    TEXT
Alt-4    TEXT
Alt-5    TEXT
Alt-6    TEXT
Alt-7    TEXT
Alt-8    TEXT
Alt-9    TEXT
Alt-0    TEXT

▶ _      ↑/↓ Select  R Revise  L Load  S Save  C Clear  ESC Exit


                            META KEYS
```

- *Figure 14.1: Two new macros*

STEP 14

SAVING YOUR MACROS

Save your Meta key definitions to make them available in later sessions. Press s for save. The definitions will be saved to the standard macro file PCPLUS.KEY.

CREATING ALTERNATE META KEYS

You can create alternate sets of Meta key definitions by bringing up the Meta key window, pressing l (ell) for load, and entering a file base-name (i.e., without the extension) of up to eight characters. When you save these definitions, they will be saved to the new file.

Selecting a set of Meta keys

When you have more than one set of definitions, you can pick one of them from the Meta key window by pressing l, pressing Enter, highlighting the name of your choice, and pressing Enter once again.

TRYING OUT YOUR MACROS

To remove the macro window, press Esc. Dial CompuServe; when the User ID prompt appears, press Alt-1 to enter your ID. Finish logging on as usual. At the main ! prompt, press Alt-2 to bring up the IBM File Finder.

Using Scripts

For almost every action you can make in PROCOMM PLUS, there is an equivalent written command that the program can read and perform on its own. When you place one or more of these commands in a text file, you have created a *script* that you can use to automate some of your online operations.

What is a script?

As you will learn in this Step and the next, you can set up a script to run when you start PROCOMM PLUS, when you dial an entry, or when you are in the midst of a session. Furthermore, you can write a script yourself or let PROCOMM PLUS monitor your transactions and write the script for you (with some limitations).

This small book can include only a sample of available PROCOMM PLUS script commands (called ASPECT commands). Try to have a copy of the *ASPECT Script Language Reference Manual* (supplied with your documentation) open as you work through this and Step 16.

CREATING A LOGON SCRIPT

You may find more use for logon scripts than for any other kind of script, because you use a logon sequence so often—yet it may be hard to remember.

87

STEP 15

A logon script can be written in *record mode*. Try using this function to write your first script.

Creating the Script

At the terminal-mode screen, press Alt-R to turn on recording. Enter the script file base-name **compu**. Press Alt-D, highlight your CompuServe dialing entry, and press Enter to dial. When you are connected, press Enter and then respond as usual to the host name, user ID, and password prompts. Before making an entry at the first menu, press Alt-R a second time to turn off recording.

While you are logged on, go to the mail section and send yourself a brief test message as you did for Step 10; you will use it in the next Step. Log off the system when you are done.

Viewing a script

View your new creation by pressing Alt-V and entering **compu.asp**. You should see something like this:

```
;
; PROCOMM PLUS generated ASPECT script
file-Editing may be required.
;
proc main
    waitfor "^M^J"
    pause 1
    transmit "^M"
    waitfor "Host Name:  "
    pause 1
    transmit "cis^M"
    waitfor "User ID: "
    pause 1
    transmit "12345,678^M"
    waitfor "Password: "
    pause 1
    transmit "first:second^M"
endproc
```

STEP 15

This script shows you a succession of three common ASPECT commands (ASPECT is the name of the PROCOMM PLUS script-file language): **waitfor, pause,** and **transmit**. The **pause** command is simplest—it tells PROCOMM PLUS to wait for the specified number of seconds (the argument of **pause**) after completing the preceding command before performing the next one. Here, it allows time for a remote system to prepare for new input.

Commands in a script

The **waitfor** and **transmit** commands take *string* arguments—that is, sequences of characters enclosed in quotes. As you see, the strings can include control characters, represented by a caret followed by another character. For instance, the argument of the first **waitfor** command represents a carriage return ("^M") and a line feed ("^J"). When PROCOMM PLUS encounters a **waitfor** command in a script, it halts until the remote system sends text that matches the argument string (or until a certain time has elapsed, as described in the *ASPECT Script Language Reference Manual*). When PROCOMM PLUS encounters a **transmit** command in a script, it sends the string argument to the remote system.

Words following a semicolon (like the top three lines) are *comments* that document the purpose and workings of the script for you. PROCOMM PLUS ignores them.

As you see, the script recorded a dialog between you and the remote computer: it first captured an incoming carriage return and line feed (which you probably didn't notice) and then your apparent response, a carriage return. It continued recording the rest of the exchange.

How the script works

Note that the script recorded nothing of your dialing sequence. Record mode does not capture local PROCOMM PLUS commands, such as calling up the dialing directory or a menu of file-transfer protocols. You must incorporate ASPECT language forms of these commands into a script by hand.

Using Scripts 89

Using the Script

To put this logon script to use, press Alt-D and highlight your CompuServe entry. Press **r** for Revise and press Enter until you reach the SCRIPT field. Enter the base name (the characters before the extension) of the script, **compu**. Continue pressing Enter until the revision is complete.

You can use the new script at once. Press Enter to dial CompuServe and watch the script at work. When you have connected to the service and returned to the terminal-mode screen, PROCOMM PLUS *compiles* the script; that is, it converts the text file into a form that it can read and act on much more rapidly. A message box to this effect appears in the middle of the screen. Note that the name of the compiled script file, COMPU.ASX, appears in the message box on the status line while the script is operating. The next time you dial CompuServe, PROCOMM PLUS will call the compiled script at once.

If you need to terminate a script while it is running, first press Esc and then **y** to confirm.

To make the new script available from any directory, copy the .ASP and .ASX files to your PCPLUS home directory and delete the originals.

USING READY-MADE SCRIPTS

PROCOMM PLUS comes packaged with a number of script files, most of them logon scripts. Take a few moments to explore a few of them. Use your file browser or editor to locate files in your PROCOMM PLUS home directory with the .ASP extension. You will find them useful examples of script programming. Try, for instance, BJACK.ASP, which demonstrates ASPECT screen handling and computation as it engages you in a game of blackjack, or try PORTS.ASP, which supplies information about your serial-port settings. Both of these scripts are designed to be run from the

90 *Up & Running with PROCOMM PLUS*

terminal-mode screen. Run each by pressing Alt-F5 and entering its name.

You can find other worthwhile ASPECT scripts in the library sections of the Datastorm CompuServe forum.

More scripts

STEP 15

Using Scripts 91

Writing Your Own Scripts

This Step illustrates a few ways to make better, more flexible script files. To begin with, try out some suggestions for improving scripts produced through the record mode.

FINE-TUNING YOUR SCRIPT

Use PCEDIT or your favorite editor to edit the script file from the previous Step, COMPU.ASP. If you use PCEDIT, make sure Setup Option A is set to read ASPECT. As noted in the comments, editing may be required; the automatically generated script is not as flexible and dependable as it could be.

Consider the first **waitfor** command. This sets up a tricky timing relationship between the carriage return/line feed sent by the local network node and the execution of the script; the characters may arrive before the script even begins. Remove this command and edit the following **pause** command to read

Removing unneeded Waitfors

```
pause 3
```

to allow the needed time and flexibility. You can delete a single line using PCEDIT by moving the cursor to that line and pressing Alt-D.

STEP 16

Using define statements

Scripts become more readable and easier to keep up to date when strings like your user ID are defined as meaningful names near the top of the file. (This is especially true if strings are used more than once.) For instance, you can define your user ID simply by adding this line above the **proc main** statement:

`define myid "12345,678"`

using your own CompuServe ID. Using PCEDIT, you can add this line by moving the cursor to the line **proc main**, pressing Ctrl-I, and typing the text. Then, for the command

`transmit "12345,678"`

substitute

`transmit myid`

In this case, you can simply backspace over the string and quotes and type in **myid**.

The full worth of substitutions such as these will become apparent when you must write a long script in which a changeable value appears several times.

Password protection

You may not wish to include your password in a script that anyone can run. An alternative is to have the script prompt you for input when the system requests a password. To do this, replace the final **transmit** command—by moving to the line, pressing Alt-D, and pressing Ctrl-I—and type these lines:

```
sound 500 50
mget s1
transmit s1
transmit "^m"
```

The idea behind this sequence of commands is to get your attention when it's time to enter a password, accept the password (without echoing it literally), and pass it on to the service. The **sound** command with these arguments produces a 500 Hz beep for about half a second. The **mget** command is a variant of **get**, which accepts keyboard input into a variable and echoes it to the local screen, without sending it to the remote system. **Mget** echoes asterisks to the screen instead of what you type; this is for security. When you type your password and press Enter, **mget** finishes and the **transmit s1** command sends the password. The second **transmit** command sends the carriage return that completes the entry.

Having made these changes, you can edit the title to read

    ; Custom-made CompuServe logon script

or something else to your liking.

The script title

USING A STARTUP SCRIPT

You may sometimes want PROCOMM PLUS to perform certain actions when you start the program. You can readily write a script to perform these actions.

Try using PCEDIT to create a short script file that will call CompuServe as soon as you start PROCOMM PLUS:

1. Press Alt-A from the terminal-mode screen and enter the argument **callcs.asp** to create this file.

2. Press F1 to enter the **proc** and **endproc** statements. (This is just one of the PCEDIT macros for ASPECT commands listed under PCEDIT help.)

3. With the cursor positioned after **proc**, type **main** and press Enter. PCEDIT automatically indents the next line to help you keep the beginning and end of the **main** procedure in view.

4. Enter these lines:

        set port com1   ; use your own serial
                               ; port
        set emulation ansi
        set baudrate 2400   ; use the rate for
                               ; your CompuServe
                                 connection

Writing Your Own Scripts 95

STEP 16

```
    set databits 7          ; use the number of
                            ; data bits and
    set parity even         ; the parity setting
                            ; that you use
    mdial "482-0190" "Dialing CompuServe..."
                            ; use your CompuServe
                            ; telephone number
    execute "compu"         ; run the logon script
```

What the startup script does

Remember that all these commands should fall between the **proc main** and **endproc** statements. This script replicates some of the settings that you include in your CompuServe dialing-directory entry. It dials the number and passes control to the logon script that you created previously. The **mdial** (for manual dial) command dials the number given as its first argument, while displaying the message that follows. The **execute** command *chains* to the script given as its argument; *that is, it passes control to that script, which never returns to the original file.*

Running the startup script

Run this script by giving its name as an argument to PROCOMM PLUS to load the program:

   pcplus /fcallcs.asp

You can include this command in a batch file to run whenever you want to reach CompuServe. The script must be located either in the current directory or the PROCOMM PLUS home directory to run.

If you write and compile a script named PROFILE.ASP and put the compiled script in your PCPLUS home directory, it will run every time you start PROCOMM PLUS.

USING A RUNTIME SCRIPT

You may sometimes want to automate an operation that you perform in mid-session. For instance, suppose you want a quick way to view your electronic mail on CompuServe.

STEP 16

Use PCEDIT to create a file called "gomail.asp" that includes the lines below. This script will demonstrate some further features of the ASPECT language:

```
proc main
   transmit "go mail^m"
   waitfor "1 READ mail" 5
   pause 3
   if waitfor
      transmit "1^m"
      waitfor "0 READ ALL" 5
      pause 3
      if waitfor
         transmit "0^m"
      endif
   else
      transmit "t^m"
   endif
endproc
```

Using PCEDIT, press F2 to enter the outermost **if-endif** pair. Enter the condition **waitfor**, enter the following statements, and press F2 to enter the second, nested, **if** condition as you did the first. Press F4 to enter **else** and enter the following statement. Note how PCEDIT handles the line starts and indentation.

The **if waitfor** statement calls for performing the commands that follow (down to an **else** or an **endif**) in the event that **waitfor** evaluates to true—that is, if the string that the nearest preceding **waitfor** command was waiting for actually arrived. Your *ASPECT Script Language Reference Manual* (supplied with the documentation) shows you that a number of ASPECT commands return values, as **waitfor** does. Note that you can *nest* **if** statements; that is, include an **if** within an **if**.

This script first sends you to CompuServe's electronic mail section. There it waits for menu item 1, which only appears if you have unsaved or undeleted mail. If that item appears, the script sends the command to read all messages; otherwise it takes you

What the runtime script does

Writing Your Own Scripts   97

STEP 16

back to the TOP menu. The **pause** commands allow CompuServe a few seconds to finish writing a menu.

Running the runtime script

To run this script, press Alt-F5 while you are at a CompuServe ! prompt. Then enter the base name of the script file, **gomail**.

USING OTHER SCRIPT COMMANDS

Take a few minutes to browse through the ASPECT reference manual. Note these classes of commands, among others:

- String variables to which you can assign strings of characters. There are numerous commands for manipulating these variables (see, for instance, the commands that begin with **str**). You can use a variable wherever you use a literal string in quotes. You used one predefined variable, **s1**, in the modified CompuServe logon script above. There are ten of these variables, numbered **s0** through **s9**. You can also create a variable by assigning it a value at the beginning of a procedure.

- Numerical variables for performing integer arithmetic. There are ten predefined numerical variables, numbered **n0** through **n9**. You can also define your own integer variables.

- Floating point and long integer variables. Conversion functions are available to make conversions between string variables and any of the numerical types.

- Commands to open, close, read from, and write to DOS files.

- The **getfile** and **sendfile** commands for file transfers, using any available protocol (used in commands like **sendfile xmodem "file_to.go"**).

- Execution control statements such as **if** statements (which have appeared in previous examples), **when** statements to repeat an action as long as a condition is true, and **switch** statements to choose an action on the basis of different values that a variable may assume.

- The **suspend until** command, which allows you to specify an hour (in 24-hour format) and a minute for your script to resume, allowing you to leave the program to run unattended.

As you grow familiar with the ASPECT language, you will gain proficiency in writing scripts. A logical sequence is to outline the operations that a new script should take, add the control structures, and fill in the commands. Note that commands are shown grouped by function beginning on page 3 of the *ASPECT Script Language Reference Manual*.

Your Own Bulletin Board

PROCOMM PLUS allows you to set up a simple bulletin board, known as *host mode*. This step will guide you through its setup and use.

SETTING UP HOST MODE

You can set up host mode simply by making one set of menu selections and (optionally) by creating one or two files.

Setting Host Mode Options

To begin, bring up the Host Mode Options menu (shown with some possible values in Figure 17.1) by pressing Alt-S and then typing h. Make the following choices:

- **A– Welcome message:** Enter a brief message to greet callers as they prepare to log in.

- **B– System type:** Decide whether you want an OPEN or a CLOSED system by toggling the value of option B. On an OPEN system, callers can log on without restriction by giving a name and password of their choosing. On a CLOSED system, only callers whom you have previously

STEP 17

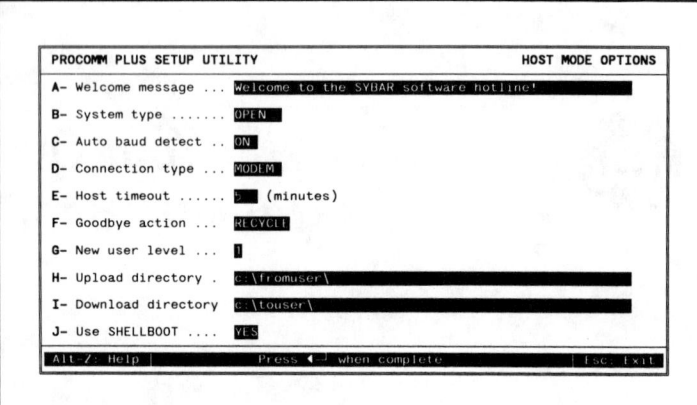

- *Figure 17.1: Host Mode Options*

   assigned IDs and passwords in the user file (discussed later) can log on.

- **C– Auto baud detect:** Leave this option ON unless your modem has difficulty lowering its speed when connecting with slower modems.

- **D– Connection type:** Set this option to MODEM to tell PROCOMM PLUS to send an auto-answer command upon entering host mode, and to wait for your modem to detect a carrier before sending the welcome message. The alternative, DIRECT, is for direct serial connection to another computer. It omits the auto-answer command and sends the welcome message immediately upon the start of host mode.

- **E– Host timeout:** Enter the number of minutes that host mode will wait for a user to type something before it hangs up.

- **F– Goodbye action:** Normally, you should leave this option set to RECYCLE so that, when one caller signs off, host mode prepares for the next. You can set the option to HANGUP if you want PROCOMM PLUS to hang up and leave host mode after a single call, or you can set it to EXIT to have the program return to the terminal mode without hanging up when the caller signs off.

- **G– New user level:** Leave this option set to 1 to allow new users the privileges accorded normal users (explained below), or set it to 0 to classify them as limited users, who are not allowed to transfer files.

- **H– Upload directory** and **I– Download directory:** Enter paths under these options to which callers may upload files and where they may look for files to download, respectively. This allows you to control access to your system and identify and review new files. Normal users (a category explained later) will have access to these directories only.

- **J– Use SHELLBOOT:** Set this option to YES to allow host mode to be restarted after a lockup has occured while a user has started a DOS shell from host mode. The full procedure is described below.

When you are done, save these settings and return to the terminal-mode screen as usual.

Creating the User File

If you are setting up a CLOSED host-mode system, you should now create a file for authorized users. Bring up your editor and edit a file called PCPLUS.USR in your PCPLUS home directory. Delete any sample entries and end-of-file marks, and add entries in this form, with fields separated by semicolons:

A closed system

`LASTNAME;FIRSTNAME;PASSWORD;1; * Comment *`

- *LASTNAME* and *FIRSTNAME* may have a combined length of 30 characters; they must appear in uppercase.

- *PASSWORD* may be up to 8 characters long; it also must be in uppercase.

- The digit that follows is 0 for a limited user, 1 for a normal user, or 2 for a privileged user, as explained later. You should designate yourself as a privileged user.

STEP 17

- The remainder of the line is available for your comment, which may extend the whole record to 80 characters total.

An open system

If you have set up an OPEN system, this file will be generated and updated automatically as users log on. You will need to edit it, however, to raise a user (such as yourself) to privileged status.

Creating the News File

You can create a file that all users read once they log on. Use your editor to create an ASCII text file called PCPLUS.NWS in your PCPLUS home directory. You can, for instance, include information about your system in this file or keep it updated with news of the day.

Creating Other Text Files

The welcome screen

You can similarly create a file called PCPLUS.NUF that is shown to new users only when they *first* log on.

The help screen

When a caller selects the Help option from the host-mode menu, he or she is shown the contents of PCPLUS.HHP, provided as part of the PROCOMM PLUS package. You can modify this file as you see fit.

About these screens

The lines in any of these files should be no wider than a PC's screen. If any of them contains more than 23 lines, PROCOMM PLUS will pause display and show the message "–MORE–" every 23 lines. Callers then press any key except Esc to view the next screenful.

Using the SHELLBOOT Feature

Sometimes a privileged user will start a DOS shell as described below, run a command whose input and output cannot be redirected from and to the remote PC, and hang up in frustration at the apparent lockup. PROCOMM PLUS provides a mechanism to reboot your computer and restart host mode in this circumstance,

104 *Up & Running with PROCOMM PLUS*

and you can put it into effect in a few quick steps:

1. Set "Use SHELLBOOT" to YES.
2. Check that the file HCOMMAND.RTE is present in your PCPLUS home directory.
3. Write a script consisting of at least these three lines, name it HOST.ASP, and compile it:

   ```
   proc main
      host
   endproc
   ```

4. Add this line to the end of your AUTOEXEC.BAT file, to start PROCOMM PLUS with the **host** command:

   ```
   pcplus /fhost
   ```

RUNNING HOST MODE

To start operation, inform potential callers of your system settings (highest transmission rate and data bit/parity setting) and press Alt-Q from the terminal-mode screen. A window will appear to show that your system is ready to receive callers.

Local Logons

To try out host mode, simulate a user's logon locally. Press F2, then press **n** in answer to the prompts:

   ```
   Continue to answer calls?
   ```

and

   ```
   Logon as SYSOP?
   ```

Enter the name and password of a hypothetical user (in the case of an open system) or of an existing normal user (in the case of a

STEP 17

closed system). You will see this menu and prompt:

```
F)iles      U)pload      D)ownload
H)elp       T)ime        C)hat
R)ead mail  L)eave mail  G)oodbye

Your choice?
```

Try some of these options, selected by pressing the initial letter. In brief, here is how they work:

Explaining the options

- Choose **Files** to see the files in the download directory. Select them by entering a file spec.

- Users picking **Upload** are prompted successively to choose a file-transfer protocol (by pressing another initial letter), to enter a file name or file spec, and to enter a brief description. They can then kick off their end of the transfer. You saw how this works in Step 8. This option is not available during a local logon.

- Users picking **Download** are prompted as for an upload, minus the description. This option is likewise not available during a local logon.

- Choose **Help** to view the help file described above.

- Choose **Time** to see the current time, as well as the time that you made the connection.

- Users can choose **Chat** to sound a bell at the host-mode system. The system operator (or anyone present there) can then press F1 to put that system in chat mode (similar to the chat mode described in Step 5) to have an exchange with a user. This function is not available for a local logon.

- Choose **Read mail** to read messages. You will be given a branching set of selections:

    — To read messages addressed to you sequentially ("Forward read")

- To read only new messages addressed to you ("New mail")
- To read messages that include in their headers a word or phrase you'll be prompted to enter next ("Search mail")
- To view a message by its number ("Individual read")

After you've read a message, you can choose to write a reply, mark a message for deletion, scroll through all further messages, or exit the mail, using a similar menu.

■ Choose **Leave mail** to send a message. You will be prompted to supply a recipient and a subject, and to make the message public or private. You can then enter the message, letting PROCOMM PLUS do the word-wrapping. Press Enter twice to terminate entry and make a disposition of the message from the following menu.

■ Choose **Goodbye** to log off the host-mode system. This choice will hang up the line (in the case of a real logon, but as described above for the Goodbye action menu option) and return the system to Waiting status.

Type **g** from the main menu to sign off and press F2 to perform another local logon. This time, type y at the following prompt:

The privileged-user mode

```
Logon as SYSOP?
```

Sysop (short for "system operator") is a reserved name for a particular privileged user. (You can later make a special sysop entry in the PCPLUS.USR file, in this form:

```
;SYSOP;PASSWORD;2; * Comment *
```

where *SYSOP* appears literally, the password is your choice, and the user type is 2.) When you reach the main menu, two additional lines appear:

```
S)hell
A)bort (SHUT DOWN host mode)
```

STEP 17

By choosing Shell, you place yourself at the command prompt of the host machine, where you can execute DOS commands and other programs that write to the screen, teletype-style. You can then return to the host-mode screen by entering **exit** at the DOS prompt.

By choosing Abort, you take the remote machine out of host mode. This is an advanced option that allows you to control that machine simply by:

- pressing Ctrl-D, typing in an ASPECT script command, and pressing Enter

or by

- running a script file containing commands in the form

    `transmit "^dcommand [arguments]^m"`

For instance, you can press Ctrl-D, type **host**, and then press Enter to return to host mode. These commands will not work after you have chosen Abort during a local logon, however.

To enable remote commands, option D on the Setup General Options menu must be turned ON.

You should now type **g** to log off again.

Interacting with users

As noted previously, you can chat with a user by pressing F1. The user will be notified that you have come online. Disconnect a user, if necessary, by pressing Ctrl-X.

Leaving host mode

Leave host mode by pressing Esc at any time. Press **y** to hang up the line if the system is off-hook.

BOOKKEEPING

PROCOMM PLUS offers you a useful means for keeping track of host-mode activities. Host-mode bookkeeping consists of a few

STEP 17

simple tasks:

- Maintaining the user list described previously.
- Reviewing the history file PCPLUS.HST. If you view this file with a browse utility, you will find that it contains a record of when callers logged on and off, and of their online activities.
- Reviewing the record of uploads PCPLUS.ULD. This file includes the names of uploaded files, the dates and times of their uploads, and the descriptions offered by their senders.
- Reviewing the mail, described below.

Invoke the program PCMAIL from the DOS prompt to work with the message database. From the main menu, you can choose to review messages, add messages, compress the message base, or quit by typing an initial letter. Reviewing messages works like reading mail when online with host mode, except that you can turn the "Deleted" and "Private" flags on and off for each message by pressing **d** or **p** at the messsage prompt. Adding messages works just like leaving mail in host mode.

Reviewing messages

To physically remove messages marked for deletion, press **c** for Compress Message Base from the main menu. Press **y** to confirm. You can then return to the DOS prompt by pressing **q** for Quit.

Your Own Bulletin Board 109

Using External Programs

You may wish that you could call up programs such as your own file browser and editor or word processor from within PROCOMM PLUS to have their sophisticated, yet familiar, features at hand online. In fact, as you will learn in this Step, you can readily make them available at the press of an Alt-key combination. You can also run commands from the DOS prompt without interrupting your PROCOMM PLUS session.

Note that PROCOMM PLUS's own file browser and editor, being simple, make modest requirements of disk space and memory. If either of these resources is in short supply, consider sticking with the means provided by PROCOMM PLUS instead of using third-party software.

MAKING THE SETTINGS

From the terminal-mode screen, first press Alt-S and then **f** to bring up the File/Path Options menu. The options of interest are D and E. They are shown with sample settings in Figure 18.1. These options are conveniently designated as an editor and a browse utility, respectively.

STEP 18

```
┌─────────────────────────────────────────────────────────────────────┐
│ PROCOMM PLUS SETUP UTILITY                      FILE/PATH OPTIONS   │
│ A- Default filename for log files (Alt-F1)                          │
│    PCPLUS.LOG                                                       │
│ B- Default filename for screen snapshot files (Alt-G)               │
│    PCPLUS.SCR                                                       │
│ C- Default path for downloaded files (PgDn)                         │
│    D:\TEMP\                                                         │
│ D- Program name for editor hot key (Alt-A)                          │
│    ED                                                               │
│ E- Program name for view utility hot key (Alt-V)                    │
│    LIST                                                             │
│                                                                     │
│                                                                     │
│                                                                     │
│ Alt-Z: Help │ Press the letter of the option to change: │ Esc: Exit │
└─────────────────────────────────────────────────────────────────────┘
```

■ *Figure 18.1: Options for external programs*

Your Own Editor

Choosing your editor

Press **d** and enter the name by which you invoke your editor or word processor. Include any arguments that you always include and that precede any optional arguments. If the editor is not on your DOS PATH, precede its name with a full path name.

About PC-Write

The name that appears in Figure 18.1, "ED," invokes the popular shareware word processor called PC-Write. This is a most useful program for communications, because it can read many kinds of document files and make many necessary conversions. For instance, it includes a simple key sequence (Alt-F4, F6, F10) that removes all special control and extended characters from a file, yielding a file in ASCII format that almost any system can read.

Loading your editor

To test this entry, drop back to the terminal-mode screen, saving the changed entry as you go. Bring up your editor by pressing Alt-A (the assigned hotkey for option D) and entering a filename parameter in response to the prompt. When you terminate the program, you are returned to the terminal-mode screen. Press Alt-S and **f** again for the File/Path Options menu.

STEP 18

Your Own File Browser

Enter the name of your file browser under option E as you entered that of your editor under option D. Again, return to the terminal-mode screen to try it out, this time by pressing Alt-V (the assigned hotkey for option E) and entering a file-name parameter.

Choosing your file browser

Figure 18.1 shows the name for the LIST file-browse utility that you may have obtained while following Step 11. If you bring up a recent version of LIST with no argument or a directory-name argument, it will show you all the files in a directory. You can then highlight a file and view it by pressing Enter.

Pressing Alt-H while viewing a file shows you that file in *hex format*, with the hexadecimal value of each character on the left and its pictorial representation on the right. (Even line endings appear as characters.) This makes the program invaluable as a diagnostic tool for files that you are transferring. Figure 18.2, for instance, shows part of an ASCII file. You can see that each line ends in a carriage return and a line feed—the values 0D and 0A—corresponding to the musical note and reverse-video O-shaped characters on the right side of the screen.

Viewing in hex format

- *Figure 18.2: LIST: A hex listing*

Using External Programs 113

Other LIST features

LIST has numerous further options that you can discover by pressing F1 for help while viewing either the directory listing or the contents of a file. You should also take time to study the manual included with the package.

When you have finished browsing, return to the terminal-mode screen.

CONNECTING TO OTHER PROGRAMS

You can run any DOS program that fits into available memory using an option for the Meta keys described in Step 14. To try this feature:

1. Press Alt-M from the terminal-mode screen
2. Highlight an unused Meta key and press **r** to revise it.
3. Press the spacebar until the Meta key's type reads "PROGRAM."
4. Press Tab and enter your chosen command as you would invoke it from the DOS prompt, including any arguments that you use.
5. Press **s** to save the new definition and press Esc to remove the window.

Run the program by pressing the Meta key itself (for instance, Alt-1) from the terminal-mode screen. When the program has run, press any key to return to PROCOMM PLUS, as prompted.

Choosing a program

The choices of programs to run are yours. Some useful choices might include:

- a viewer for graphic images such as CompuServe GIF files
- an archiving program such as PKZIP to prepare files for uploading
- a file-finder program such as the one included with Norton Utilities

THE DOS GATEWAY

To start DOS without terminating PROCOMM PLUS, press Alt-F4 from the terminal-mode screen. (This is often called "shelling to DOS.") You can then run any programs that fit within remaining memory. When you are ready to return to your PROCOMM PLUS session, enter the command **exit** at the DOS prompt.

Using Terminal Emulation

Computer terminals don't have the intimate connection with a mainframe computer that your PC's keyboard and video circuits have with their system unit. Since terminals are connected only by communication lines, such functions as cursor movement, screen colors, or interpretation of function and control keys must take place by means of special character sequences embedded in the data that are sent and received.

Because these sequences are not standardized among makes and models of terminals, a communications program must be able to emulate a variety of terminals. Beyond allowing you to choose among several emulations, PROCOMM PLUS allows you to modify outgoing control sequences for each emulation. It also allows you to control some general aspects of terminal emulation, such as display of character attributes. Finally, it allows you to translate any incoming character value to a different value so that you can remove or redefine characters that do not display properly.

Emulating a variety of charac- teristics

SETTING TERMINAL OPTIONS

Bring up the Terminal Options menu by pressing Alt-S and then t from the terminal-mode screen. Typical settings are shown in Figure 19.1.

STEP 19

Here is a summary of their uses:

- **A– Terminal emulation:** Choose this option to pick a computer terminal from a menu for PROCOMM PLUS to emulate at program startup. The emulation setting in your last-called dialing-directory entry will override this choice, as the entry's duplex setting will override your choice for option B.

- **B– Duplex:** Choose FULL or HALF duplex to turn the local echo of what you type OFF or ON.

- **C– Software flow control (XON/XOFF):** If a remote system sends XOFF and XON characters (ASCII control characters 19 and 17, respectively) to stop and restart the flow of data from a terminal (allowing it time to process the data), setting this option to ON will allow PROCOMM PLUS to respond by suspending transmission on receipt of an XOFF and resuming it on receipt of an XON. Otherwise, it should be left OFF to avoid problems with binary file transfers, where these characters may occur as part of the data.

- **D– Hardware flow control (RTS/CTS):** This form of flow control involving the RS-232 serial control lines called

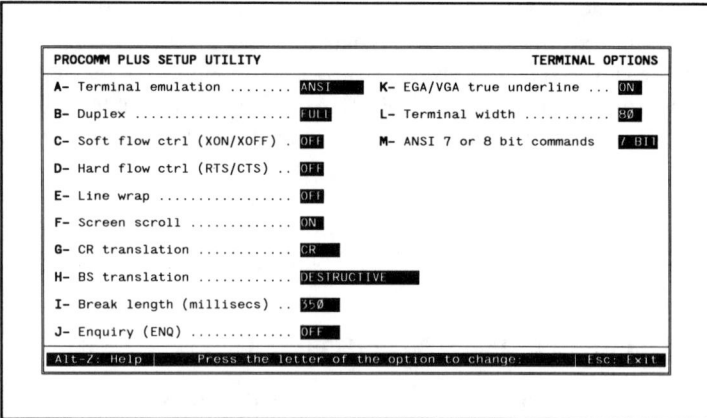

- *Figure 19.1: The Terminal Options menu*

118 *Up & Running with PROCOMM PLUS*

Request to Send (RTS) and Clear to Send (CTS) is used by some high-speed modems. PROCOMM PLUS will raise RTS to signify it has data to send, but will send them only after the modem has raised CTS. Turn this option ON only if your modem's documentation states that it is needed.

- **E– Line wrap:** Turn this option ON if you are receiving lines longer than 80 characters and want the additional characters to be shown on subsequent display lines instead of disappearing off the right margin.

- **F– Screen scroll:** Turn this option ON if you want the screen to scroll. Otherwise, the remote system will have to send a control sequence to clear the screen between each screenful of text.

- **G– CR translation:** If the remote system sends carriage returns without line feeds, you will have to set this option to CR/LF to keep following lines from overwriting preceding lines. Otherwise, leave it set to CR.

- **H– BS translation:** Set this option to NON-DESTRUCTIVE if a terminal, upon receipt of a backspace character, would normally just move the cursor left one column without erasing the character there.

- **I– Break length (milliseconds):** Some remote systems respond to a break signal—that is, a sustained zero value sent by the terminal—by initiating one action or another. This option sets the exact length of the break signal PROCOMM PLUS will send when you press Alt-B from the terminal-mode screen.

- **J– Enquiry (ENQ):** Settings for this option determine whether PROCOMM PLUS will perform some special action upon receiving an ASCII 5 character, designated the Enquiry character (ENQ for short). With the setting ON, PROCOMM PLUS will send the Meta key text macro that you have assigned to the Alt-0 key. (Some remote systems expect an identification sequence in reply when they send ENQ. If you communicate with such a system, you can learn the sequence required and assign it to this macro.) With the setting CIS B, PROCOMM PLUS will initiate a

STEP 19

download using the CompuServe B protocol whenever CompuServe sends this character.

- **K– EGA/VGA true underline:** If you have an EGA or VGA display, you can turn this option ON so that incoming text with an underline attribute shows a real underline.

- **L– Terminal width:** You can set this to 80 or 132 columns. If you choose the 132-column setting (and if the remote system is sending 132-column text), you will ordinarily see little more than half the width of the screen at any one time. PROCOMM PLUS will show you the side of the screen currently occupied by the cursor, but you can manually switch the display by pressing Ctrl-→ or Ctrl-←. (If you have an advanced video display, you can set up PROCOMM PLUS to display a true 132 columns. This technique is detailed in my *Understanding PROCOMM PLUS*.)

- **M– ANSI 7 or 8 bit commands:** You can leave this option set to 7 BIT, or set it to 8 BIT to allow PROCOMM PLUS to interpret command sequences used by some advanced DEC terminals.

SETTING TERMINAL COLOR OPTIONS

Reach this menu from the preceding one by pressing Esc, **c**, and then **t**. Remote systems send special character sequences to control how text is displayed on a terminal (its color or its attribute—such as reverse video—on a monochrome terminal). This menu (shown in Figure 19.2) determines how PROCOMM PLUS translates sequences for monochrome attributes, as well as how it writes its messages to the terminal-mode screen. Color attributes are simply displayed as sent.

If you have a color display

Try this sequence of steps for mapping monochrome terminal attributes to be displayed on your color monitor:

1. Press **a** to begin setting your normal text attribute.

2. From the window that appears, use the arrow keys or the mouse to select a new color attribute by number by

120 *Up & Running with PROCOMM PLUS*

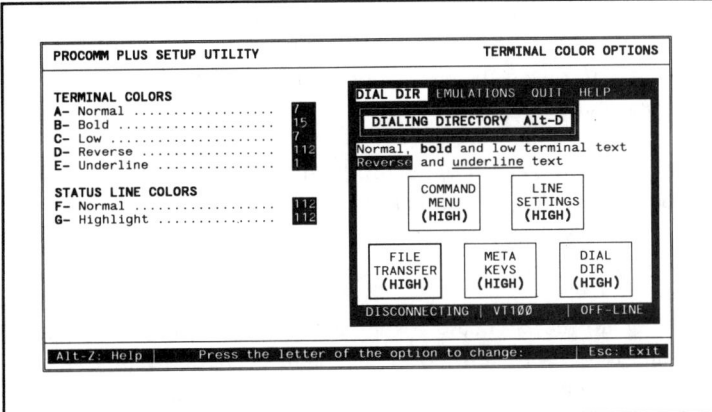

- *Figure 19.2: The Terminal Color Options menu*

   positioning a box around the number. Note the effect of the new attribute on the sample screen at the right. For instance, select box **23** to give normal text the attribute of gray-on-blue. Press Enter when you are satisfied.

3. Repeat steps 1 and 2 for the other attribute letters to pick useful colors for other terminal attributes, as well as for your status-line colors. Note that the underline attribute must be blue-on-black to display a real underline.

4. When you are done, press Esc twice and then press Enter to save your changes.

You can make standard settings for a black-and-white screen by starting PROCOMM PLUS with the /b flag, bringing up the Terminal Colors menu, and saving and exiting setup as usual.

If you have a black-and-white display

CHANGING KEYBOARD MAPPINGS

Under a PROCOMM PLUS terminal emulation, the regular letter, number, and punctuation keys send their respective characters (unshifted or shifted), but various keypad and function keys are mapped to specialized keys on the terminal being emulated, and so are programmed to send character sequences that the corresponding

STEP 19

keys on that terminal would generate. You can reassign different sequences to these keypad and function keys. You will have to determine if this is necessary or helpful in conjunction with a remote system that you use.

For key mapping to work, the program PCKEYMAP.EXE must be in your PCPLUS home directory. You can bring up this program either from within PROCOMM PLUS (as described below) or from the DOS command line.

To bring up the keyboard-mapping menu, press Alt-F8 from the terminal-mode screen. Find the terminal emulation that you want to modify by pressing the spacebar or PgUp/PgDn. (Use the PgUp and PgDn keys on the numeric keypad, with NumLock OFF.) Figure 19.3 shows the screen for the ANSI emulation.

Changing the mapping

To change a definition, press the key (or key combination, such as Ctrl-F10) that you want to redefine. Enter the new value. Use the appropriate case for letters of the alphabet in the definition and use the caret-character notation to represent a control character—as, for instance, ^M for carriage return, ^H for backspace, or ^[for Esc. Turn NumLock ON to change keys on the numeric keypad. Note that you can't redefine the PgUp or PgDn values on the numeric keypad because they are appropriated for program control.

```
         PROCOMM PLUS          F1  .....  ^[OP     S-F1  ....  ^[OR     C-F1
       KEYBOARD MAPPING        F2  .....  ^[OQ     S-F2  ....  ^[OS     C-F2
          Version 2.0          F3  .....  ^[Ow     S-F3  ....  ^[Oy     C-F3
                               F4  .....  ^[Ox     S-F4  ....  ^[Om     C-F4
                               F5  .....  ^[Ot     S-F5  ....  ^[Ov     C-F5
KEYPAD *   *                   F6  .....  ^[Ou     S-F6  ....  ^[Ol     C-F6
KEYPAD -   -                   F7  .....  ^[Oq     S-F7  ....  ^[Oa     C-F7
KEYPAD +   +                   F8  .....  ^[Or     S-F8  ....  ^[OM     C-F8
KEYPAD .   .                   F9  .....  ^[Op     S-F9  ....  ^[On     C-F9
KEYPAD /   /                   F10 ....  ^[Op     S-F10 ...  ^[OM     C-F10
KEY ENTER ^M                   F11 ....           S-F11 ...           C-F11
                               F12 ....           S-F12 ...           C-F12

TAB ......  ^I       KEYPAD 0  0        GREY CUP    ^[[A       CURUP    ^[[A
BACKTAB ...          KEYPAD 1  1        GREY CDN    ^[[B       CURDN    ^[[B
INSERT ....          KEYPAD 2  2        GREY CLF    ^[[D       CURLF    ^[[D
DELETE ....  «D»     KEYPAD 3  3        GREY CRT    ^[[C       CURRT    ^[[C
BACKSPACE .  ^H      KEYPAD 4  4        GREY INS
C-HOME ....  ^[[L    KEYPAD 5  5        GREY DEL    «D»        HOME     ^[[H
C-END .....          KEYPAD 6  6        GREY HOME   ^[[H       END      ^[[K
C-PGUP ....  ^[[M    KEYPAD 7  7        GREY END    ^[[K
C-PGDN ....  ^[[H^[[2J KEYPAD 8  8      GREY PGUP              ENTER    ^M
C-BACKSPACE  «D»     KEYPAD 9  9        GREY PGDN
 ANSI        PgUp/Dn:Terminals     Alt-O:Open    Alt-S:Save   Esc:Exit    PCPLUS KBD
```

▪ *Figure 19.3: A keyboard-mapping menu*

STEP 19

To learn how to enter a Ctrl-^ (ASCII 30) or DEL (ASCII 127) character as part of a definition, see the context-sensitive help screens for this menu.

When you are finished making changes, press Esc. Press **y** to save changes and make them available, or **n** to abandon them. Changes go into a single file, PCPLUS.KEY, located in your PCPLUS home directory.

Saving the changes

TRANSLATING INCOMING CHARACTERS

PROCOMM PLUS allows you to make a setting to translate incoming characters of a given ASCII value to any other ASCII value. You can also completely filter out characters of any given value. This feature allows you to remove nuisance characters sent by a given system. These settings are made to a PROCOMM PLUS entity called the *translation table*.

The translation table

Bring up the translation table by pressing Alt-W from the terminal-mode screen. As shown in Figure 19.4, this table consists of pairs of ASCII values. The left-hand member of the table is the incoming value and the right-hand member is the translated value. Initially, all characters are translated to themselves.

```
                    ┤ TRANSLATION TABLE ├
     0:   0    16: 16    32: 32    48: 48    64: 64    80: 80    96: 96    112:112
     1:   1    17: 17    33: 33    49: 49    65: 65    81: 81    97: 97    113:113
     2:   2    18: 18    34: 34    50: 50    66: 66    82: 82    98: 98    114:114
     3:   3    19: 19    35: 35    51: 51    67: 67    83: 83    99: 99    115:115
     4:   4    20: 20    36: 36    52: 52    68: 68    84: 84    100:100   116:116
     5:   5    21: 21    37: 37    53: 53    69: 69    85: 85    101:101   117:117
     6:   6    22: 22    38: 38    54: 54    70: 70    86: 86    102:102   118:118
     7:   7    23: 23    39: 39    55: 55    71: 71    87: 87    103:103   119:119
     8:   8    24: 24    40: 40    56: 56    72: 72    88: 88    104:104   120:120
     9:   9    25: 25    41: 41    57: 57    73: 73    89: 89    105:105   121:121
    10: 10    26: 26    42: 42    58: 58    74: 74    90: 90    106:106   122:122
    11: 11    27: 27    43: 43    59: 59    75: 75    91: 91    107:107   123:123
    12: 12    28: 28    44: 44    60: 60    76: 76    92: 92    108:108   124:124
    13: 13    29: 29    45: 45    61: 61    77: 77    93: 93    109:109   125:125
    14: 14    30: 30    46: 46    62: 62    78: 78    94: 94    110:110   126:126
    15: 15    31: 31    47: 47    63: 63    79: 79    95: 95    111:111   127:127

      F1▶ Save    F2▶ Toggle Screens    F3▶ Table On    F4▶ Table Off    ESC▶ Exit
                             Translation Table INACTIVE
                      NUMBER TO CHANGE ──▶ _    NEW VALUE ──▶
```

- *Figure 19.4: The translation table*

STEP 19

Translating a character

The table initially shows the first 128 characters of the full character set. To see the second 128, press F2. Press F2 a second time to return to the first set.

To translate a character, first enter the old value and then enter the translated value. To filter out a character, make the second value 0. For instance, enter **7** and then **0** to filter out all incoming ASCII 7 (bell) characters. Save the modified table by pressing F1. (This modifies a file named PCPLUS.XLT in your PCPLUS home directory.) Press F3 to make the table active or F4 to render it inactive. Press Esc to return to the terminal-mode screen.

You can also turn the translation table ON or OFF by setting option E in the Setup General Options menu. This option offers the further setting STRIP, which, when made, clears the high bit from all incoming characters, translating all high-ASCII characters to their 7-bit equivalents.

Customizing Your System

This final Step covers options affecting the general appearance and operation of PROCOMM PLUS. These options include screen dimensions, window colors, and operation of menus and windows; they appear in three setup menus.

MODIFYING DISPLAY/SOUND OPTIONS

Reach the Display/Sound Options screen shown in Figure 20.1 by pressing Alt-S and then **d** from the terminal-mode screen. Here are brief descriptions of these options:

- **A– Exploding windows:** Set this option ON for the characteristic PROCOMM PLUS windows that appear to jump from the screen.

- **B– Sound effects:** This option controls the sounds that accompany the appearance and disappearance of PROCOMM PLUS windows. Set it to ON to allow these sounds.

- **C– Alarm sound:** This option controls the beeping that happens when PROCOMM PLUS connects with a remote system, completes a file transfer, or receives a page from a host mode user.

STEP 20

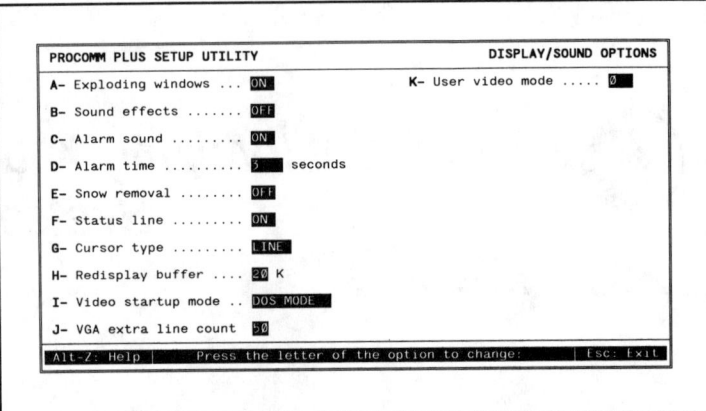

- *Figure 20.1: Display/Sound Options*

- **D– Alarm time:** Enter a time in seconds for the alarm to sound, if you have set it ON for option C.

- **E– Snow removal:** Turn this option ON to eliminate the white flecks that may appear on some older CGA adapters when PROCOMM PLUS is writing to the screen. This choice may also improve screen writing to some video adapters that are not very PC-compatible. Otherwise, leave it OFF for faster display.

- **F– Status line:** Turn the terminal-mode status line OFF here to add one more line to your terminal emulation (to have, for instance, 25 lines instead of 24). You can display or remove the status line from the terminal-mode screen itself by pressing Ctrl-].

- **G– Cursor type:** Leave this option set to LINE for an ordinary narrow cursor that underscores a character, or set it to BLOCK to have a cursor at full character height.

- **H– Redisplay buffer:** This option determines how much data can be saved for redisplay when you press Alt-F6, as described in Step 13.

- **I– Video startup mode:** This option offers you a variety of dimension settings for the PROCOMM PLUS screen;

however, you need the proper video hardware to take advantage of them:

— Set the option to DOS MODE to tell PROCOMM PLUS to use the screen dimensions that it finds upon start-up. You must start PROCOMM PLUS while in a text mode of at least 80 columns by 25 lines for this to work.

— Set it to 25 X 80 to force PROCOMM PLUS to start with 80 columns by 25 lines, the usual dimensions.

— Set it to EXTRA X 80 to start with 80 columns by the number of lines that you have set in option J on a VGA adapter, or by 43 lines on an EGA adapter.

— Set it to USER MODE to use the video mode you have set for option K.

— Set it to EXTRA X USER to use the option K setting, but to increase the line count to the value for option J.

You can cycle through the choices available for your video system directly from the terminal-mode screen by pressing the Toggle lines command key, Ctrl- –.

- **J– VGA extra line count:** Set this option to 28, 43, or 50 to display that number of lines of text on your VGA adapter.

- **K– User video mode:** Have PROCOMM PLUS use one of your video adapter's special text modes by entering its number here. See my *Understanding PROCOMM PLUS* for more information on using this feature.

MODIFYING GENERAL OPTIONS

Bring up the Setup General Options menu by pressing Alt-S and then **g** from the terminal-mode screen. Each of the options in this menu (Figure 20.2) is summarized in the accompanying help

Customizing Your System 127

STEP 20

screens. Here are a few notes on these options:

- **A– Print device:** If your printer is connected to a port other than LPT1 (PRN), you can enter that port here, as by typing COM2 or LPT2.

- **B– CD high at exit:** This setting tells PROCOMM PLUS what to do when the Carrier Detect line is high when you press Alt-X to exit the program. It can IGNORE the fact and exit anyhow (allowing you to restart the program later without having lost your connection), HANGUP automatically, or ASK you if you want to hang up, as it does by default.

- **C– Enhanced kb speedup:** You can set this option ON to set your enhanced keyboard to produce repeated characters faster and with less initial delay as you hold a key down.

- **D– Remote commands:** You can turn this option ON to enable remote commands, as described in Step 17.

- **E– Translation table:** Setting this option ON puts the translation table described in Step 19 into effect. This is also what happens when you press F3 with the table itself onscreen. Setting the option to STRIP simply clears the

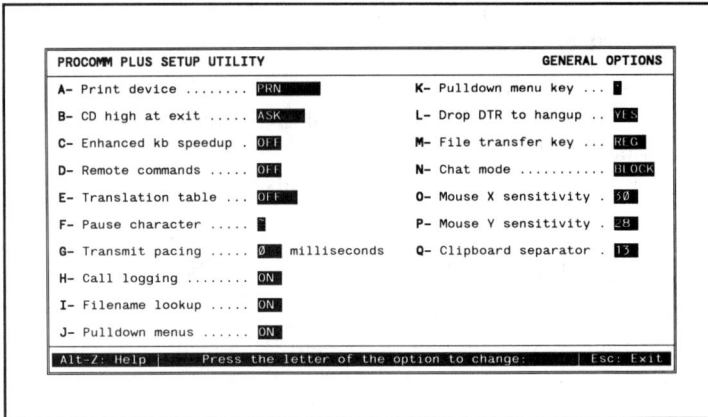

- *Figure 20.2: Setup General Options*

128 *Up & Running with PROCOMM PLUS*

high bits on all incoming characters, an effect similar to setting SPACE parity.

- **F– Pause character:** Enter the character that you put into modem commands and macros to tell PROCOMM PLUS to insert a half-second pause. You are unlikely to have to change this from the default character, a tilde.

- **G– Transmit pacing:** This option specifies an interval in milliseconds that PROCOMM PLUS inserts between characters in keyboard macros, modem commands, and sequences of characters that are assigned to keys under a terminal emulation. The default value for this option is 0 for no pause; you can enter a value of up to 999 (nearly one second) if either your modem or a given remote system needs more time to process each character in any of these sequences.

- **H– Call logging:** Turn this option ON to have PROCOMM PLUS maintain the call log (PCPLUS.FON) described in Step 13.

- **I– Filename lookup:** If you turn this option ON, PROCOMM PLUS will attempt to supply a file name when you start a file transfer by searching the screen for a sequence of characters that fits DOS naming conventions (i.e., up to eight legal characters, a period, and up to three more legal characters). It will use the last such sequence that it finds. You can then easily replace this name with a correct one, if necessary.

- **J– Pulldown menus:** Turn this option ON to use the Windows-style topline menu described in Step 2. You can turn it OFF if you do not use this menu or if you have no keyboard character to spare as its hotkey (designated by option K).

- **K– Pulldown Menu key:** Enter the letter, number, or punctuation character that you want to dedicate to bringing up the Lotus-style topline menu. Uppercase characters are distinguished from lowercase characters for this purpose.

Customizing Your System

STEP 20

- **L– Drop DTR to hangup:** Normally, dropping the Data Terminal Ready serial line is the fastest way to make a modem hang up. If your modem doesn't respond to this action in the intended way—for instance, if it resets itself—you can set this option to NO and rely on the hangup command given in the Modem Command Options menu to tell the modem to hang up.

- **M– File transfer key:** Change these keys from PgUp and PgDn to Ctrl-PgUp and Ctrl-PgDn if you need the original keystrokes for something else.

- **N– Chat mode:** Leave this setting at BLOCK to have what you type sent to someone at the other end of your connection line by line, or set it to CHAR to have it sent character by character. Note that what you type in host-mode chat mode is always sent character by character.

- **O– Mouse X sensitivity** and **P– Mouse Y sensitivity:** Specify lower or higher numbers for these options to make your mouse more or less sensitive on the X (left-right) or Y (up-down) axis.

- **Q– Clipboard separator:** Specify the ASCII decimal value of a character to send between file names when you paste the names from the clipboard (mentioned in Step 7). Use the character required by a particular service. For instance, enter 13 to use a carriage return, or 59 to use a semicolon.

SETTING COLOR OPTIONS

You've read how to set color attributes for the terminal-mode screen in Step 19. This section covers color settings for the remaining menus and windows that are part of PROCOMM PLUS.

Reach the Window Color Options menu from the General Options menu by pressing Esc, **c**, and **w**. You can set window colors just as you set the terminal-mode attribute colors described in Step 19:

1. Press **a** to begin setting colors for your command menu (reached by pressing Alt-Z from terminal mode).

2. From the window that appears, use the arrow keys or the mouse to select a new color combination for this window by number. Press Enter when you are satisfied.

3. Repeat steps 1 and 2 for the normal and high-intensity settings of the other windows, as designated by letter. You can move freely between windows and colors using the four arrow keys. These settings apply to more windows than are actually shown as options. For instance, the Meta Key window colors also apply to the Elapsed Time and Exit windows.

   If you pick the same color for the foreground and the background (irrespective of intensity), reverse video characters become unreadable.

4. When you are done, press Esc twice and then press Enter to save your changes.

As with terminal colors, you can make standard settings for a black-and-white screen by starting PROCOMM PLUS with the /b flag, bringing up the Window Colors menu, and saving and exiting setup as usual.

Settings for a black-and-white screen

Index

A

alarm settings, 12, 125–126
alternate macros, 86
ANSI terminals, 40
archiving utilities, 47–48
arguments, 89, 112
ASCII files, 53, 59–64, 72, 112
ASPECT commands, 87–89
ATM1 command, 34
auto-answer mode, 35
auto baud detect, 102
AUTOEXEC.BAT file, 3–5

B

background color, 131
backing up disks, 1
backspace setting for emulation, 119
batch-file transfers, 68–69, 72–73
baud rate, 3, 8, 14, 26
binary files with Kermit, 72
black-and-white screen settings, 131
blocks of text, 57
bookkeeping in Host Mode, 108–109
break signals with emulation, 119
buffer, redisplay, 77–80, 126
bulletin boards
  Host Mode for, 101–109
  protocols on, 67

C

call waiting, 19
calls, logging, 82, 129
carets (^), 89
carriage returns
  in ASCII files, 64
  with emulation, 119
  in scripts, 89
Carrier DetTect (CD) line, 128
catalogs, CompuServe, 80–81
characters, translating, 123–124, 128
chat modes, 35–36, 106–107, 130
circular dialing, 31–35
clipboard setting, 130
closed Host Mode systems, 101–103
collisions, name, 74
color
  with editor, 55
  settings for, 130–131
  with terminal emulation, 120–121
COM port setting, 3, 14, 20
command-summary screen, 10–11
comments
  in Host Mode user files, 104
  in scripts, 89
CompuServe
  catalogs in, 80–81
  directory entry for, 27–28
  downloading messages from, 62–63
  exiting, 42
  forums on, 41–42
  locating files on, 43–47
  logon script for, 88–90
  navigating, 38–41
  protocols for, 45–46
  signing up for, 37–38

133

uploading messages to, 59–62
ZMODEM protocol on, 65–66
CONFIG.SYS files, 3, 5
connection status, 9
connection type, Host Mode, 102
context-sensitive help, 7, 11, 123
control characters, 89
copying blocks, 57
cursor type setting, 126
customizing PROCOMM PLUS, 125–131

D

data-bits setting, 3, 8, 14, 26
Data Carrier Detect (DCD) line, 5, 18
Data Terminal Ready (DTR) line, 5, 18, 130
date
  of calls in directories, 26
  displaying, 77–78
define script command, 94
dialing
  circular, 31–35
  codes for, 28–29
  command sequence for, 18–19
  manual, 35–36
  scripts for, 89
  setting for, 3
dialing directory, 21–29
.DIR files, 21
directories and directory entries. *See also* files
  dialing, 21–29
  download, 5
  marking, 25, 32

viewing, 49–50
Display/Sound settings, 11, 125–127
DOS
  gateway to, 115
  from Host Mode, 108
  script commands for, 98
DOS startup-mode setting, 127
downloading files, 4–5
  archiving utilities for, 47–48
  ASCII, 62–63
  from CompuServe, 42
  in Host Mode, 103, 106
  with Kermit, 74
  locating files for, 43–47
  path for, 13
  using ZMODEM, 68–69
DSZ.ZIP file, 65–69
duplex setting, 26, 35, 118

E

echoing, 35
editing
  scripts, 93–95
  text entries, 12–13
editors
  built-in, 53–57
  external, 111–112
elapsed time, 33, 77–78
else script command, 97
emulations, terminal, 8, 117–124
endif script command, 97
endproc script command, 95
enhanced kb speedup setting, 128
enquiry characters with emulation, 119–120

Enter key in macros, 84
environment variables, 65
erasing directory entries, 24–25
error detection, 51
execute script command, 96
exiting, 15
  CompuServe, 42
  from DOS gateway, 115
  editor, 57
  Host Mode, 108
exploding windows setting, 125
external programs, 111–115
external protocols, 65–69
EXTRA X 80 startup mode
    setting, 127
EXTRA X USER startup mode
    setting, 127

F

file browsers, external, 113–114
file finders, 43–47, 50
file-name lookup setting, 129
files
  ASCII, 53, 59–64, 72, 112
  binary, with Kermit, 72
  downloading (*See* downloading files)
  editing, 53–57
  in Host Mode, 106
  listing, 49–50
  log, 8, 37–38, 42, 80–81, 129
  packing, 47–48
  printing directories to, 24
  system, modifying, 4–5
  uploading (*See* uploading files)

user, in Host Mode, 102–103
files= setting, 5
filtering characters, 123–124
foreground color, 131
forums on CompuServe, 41–42

G

gateway to DOS, 115
get script command, 94–95
getfile script command, 98
goodbye action in host mode, 102–103

H

half-duplex operation, 35
hardware flow control, 118–119
help, 7, 11
  for editor, 55
  for Host Mode, 106
  for keyboard mappings, 123
hexadecimal file listings, 113
Host Mode
  bookkeeping in, 108–109
  getting into, 51
  running, 105–108
  setting up, 101–105

I

IBM File Finder, 43–47
if script command, 97–98
initializing modems, 17–18
input, variable, 94–95
insert mode, PCEDIT, 56
installation, 1–5

interactive file-transfer mode, 71
IRQ lines, 20

K

Kbd file, 26
Kermit protocol, 71–76
keyboard macros, 55, 83–86
keyboards
  enhanced, 128
  mapping, 26, 121–123
keys, editing, 12–13

L

licensing agreements, 48, 69
line feeds in scripts, 89
line-settings box, 8
line-wrap settings, 119
LIST browse utility, 66–67, 69, 113–114
loading macros, 86
local echoes, 35
local logons, 105–108
log files, 8, 37–38, 42, 80–81, 129
logging calls, 82, 129
logging off UNIX systems, 75
logon scripts, 87–90

M

macros, 55, 83–86
mail in Host Mode, 106–107, 109
manual dialing, 35–36

mapping keyboards, 26, 121–123
marking directory entries, 25, 32
mdial script command, 96
message box, 7
messages
  on CompuServe, 41–42
  downloading, 62–63
  in Host Mode, 107, 109
  uploading, 59–62
Meta files, 26
Metakeys, 55, 83–86
mget script command, 94–95
modem speaker, turning on, 34
modems
  communicating with, 17–20
  settings for, 5, 8, 14–15, 26, 72
monitor settings, 2
mouse-sensitivity setting, 130

N

name collisions, 74
navigating
  CompuServe, 38–41
  directories, 23
news files, Host Mode, 104
notes, 25, 55–56
numeric script variables, 98

O

open Host Mode systems, 101, 104
overstrike mode, PCEDIT, 56

P

pacing settings, 64, 129
packing files, 47–48
parity settings, 3, 8, 14, 26, 72
passwords
  in CompuServe, 38
  in Host Mode user files, 103
  in macros, 84
  in scripts, 94
paths, 2, 4–5, 13
pause script command, 89
pauses
  for ASCII files, 64
  character setting for, 129
  in dialing window, 33
  for file logging, 81
  in macros, 84–85
PC-Write word processor, 112
PCEDIT, 25, 53–57
pcinstal command, 2–4
PCKEYMAP.EXE file, 122
PCMAIL, 109
pcplus command, 7
PCPLUS.DIR file, 21
PCPLUS.FON file, 82
PCPLUS.HHP file, 104
PCPLUS.HST file, 109
PCPLUS.KEY file, 86
PCPLUS.NUF file, 104
PCPLUS.NWS file, 104
PCPLUS.SCR file, 80
PCPLUS.ULD file, 109
PCPLUS.USR file, 102–103
PKZIP/PKUNZIP utility, 43–48
print-device option, 128
printer status, 9
printing
  directories, 24

log files, 42
  online, 82
redisplay buffer, 80
privileged user in Host Mode, 107
proc script command, 95
program disks, backing up, 1
protocols, 4, 25
  batch transfer, 50–52
  on CompuServe, 45–46
  external, 65–69
pulldown menus, settings for, 129
pulse dialing, 3

R

ready-made scripts, 90–91
receiving files. *See* downloading files
record keeping, 77–82
record mode, 88
redisplay buffer, 77–80, 126
registering shareware, 48, 69
remote systems, 7, 128
RTS/CTS flow control, 118–119
runtime scripts, 96–98

S

saving
  editor files, 57
  macros, 86
  redisplay buffer, 79–80
  screen, 80
  setup values, 13–14
screen
  saving, 80

scrolling, 77–78, 119
scripts, 25
  in dialing window, 32
  editing, 54, 93–95
  logon, 87–90
  macros with, 55
  runtime, 96–98
  startup, 95–96
scrolling of screen, 77–78, 119
searching
  for characters in directories, 24
  for text, 56–57, 79
self-unpacking archives, 47
sendfile script command, 98
sending files. *See* uploading files
serial ports, 3, 14, 20
server file-transfer mode, 71, 74–75
settings, 11–12
  color, 130–131
  display/sound, 11, 125–127
  general, 127–130
  for modems, 5, 8, 14–15, 26, 72
  saving, 13–14
  startup, 2–3
shareware, 48, 69
shell, 107–108, 115
SHELLBOOT option in host mode, 103–105
size of redisplay buffer, 78
snapshot, screen, 80
snow-removal setting, 126
software flow control, 118
sorting directories, 25

sound-effects setting, 11, 125
sound-script command, 94
speaker, modem, turning on, 34
startup scripts, 95–96
startup settings, 2–3
status line, 7, 126
stop bits setting, 8, 26
streaming protocols, 51
strings in scripts, 89, 94, 98
suspend until script command, 99
switch script command, 98
SYSOP in Host Mode, 107
system files, modifying, 4–5
system type, Host Mode, 101–102

T

terminal mode, 7–8
terminals
  color options for, 120–121
  for CompuServe, 40
  emulation of, 8, 117–124
text, editor for, 25, 53–57
text files, 53, 59–64, 72, 112
tildes (~) for pauses, 84–85
time, displaying, 33, 77–78, 106
TIMEOUT messages, 34
timeouts in host mode, 102
tone dialing, 3
topline menu, 9–10
transfers. *See* downloading files; uploading files
translating characters, 123–124, 128

transmission-mode box, 8
transmit-pacing setting, 129
transmit-script command, 89

U

underlining with terminals, 120–121
UNIX systems, 71–75
uploading files, 49–52
  ASCII, 59–62
  in Host Mode, 103, 106, 109
  with Kermit, 72–73
user files, Host Mode, 102–103
user levels in host mode, 103
USER startup-mode seting, 127

V

variables
  environment, 65
  for scripts, 95, 98
video startup-mode settings, 126–127
viewer, 82
viewing directories, 49–50

W

waitfor script command, 89, 93, 97
welcome message, Host Mode, 101
when script command, 98
width of terminals, 121
windows, exploding, setting, 125
word-wrapping, 54, 56
WP mode, PCEDIT, 54–55

X

XMODEM protocol, 46–47, 65
XON/XOFF flow control, 118

Y

YMODEM protocols, 47, 50–52

Z

.ZIP files, 48
ZMODEM protocol, 47, 65–69

Help Yourself with Another Quality Sybex Book

The ABC's of Windows 3.1
Alan R. Neibauer

Perfect for beginners — including those who are new to computers—this book covers everything from starting the system, to using the File Manager, running applications, transferring information between windows, and more.

306pp; 7 1/2" x 9"
ISBN: 0-89588-839-4

Available at Better Bookstores Everywhere

Sybex Inc.
2021 Challenger Drive
Alameda, CA 94501
Telephone (800) 227-2346
Fax (510) 523-2373

Sybex. Help Yourself.

Help Yourself with Another Quality Sybex Book

Mastering Windows 3.1
Robert Cowart

The complete guide to installing, using, and making the most of Windows on IBM PCs and compatibles now in an up-to-date new edition. Part I provides detailed, hands-on coverage of major Windows features that are essential for day-to-day use. Part II offers complete tutorials on the accessory programs. Part III explores a selection of advanced topics.

600pp; 7 1/2" x 9"
ISBN: 0-89588-842-4

Available
at Better
Bookstores
Everywhere

 Sybex Inc.
2021 Challenger Drive
Alameda, CA 94501
Telephone (800) 227-2346
Fax (510) 523-2373

Sybex. Help Yourself.

Help Yourself with Another Quality Sybex Book

Supercharging Windows
Judd Robbins

Here's a gold mine of answers to common questions, with details on undocumented features, optimization, and advanced capabilities. This book's wide-ranging topics include Windows for laptops, programming language interfacing, memory-resident software, and networking—just to name a few. Includes two disks full of productivity tools, utilities, games, and accessories.

1011pp; 71/2" x9"
ISBN: 0-89588-862-9

Available at Better Bookstores Everywhere

 Sybex Inc.
2021 Challenger Drive
Alameda, CA 94501
Telephone (800) 227-2346
Fax (510) 523-2373

Sybex. Help Yourself.

Help Yourself with Another Quality Sybex Book

Mastering Microsoft Word for Windows
Version 2.0 Second Edition
Michael J. Young

Available at Better Bookstores Everywhere

Here is an up-to-date new edition of our complete guide to Word for Windows, featuring the latest software release. It offers a tutorial for newcomers, and hands-on coverage of intermediate to advanced topics with desktop publishing skills emphasized. Special topics include: tables and columns, fonts, graphics, Styles and Templates, macros, and multiple windows.

596pp; 7 1/2" x 9"
ISBN: 0-7821-1012-6

Sybex Inc.
2021 Challenger Drive
Alameda, CA 94501
Telephone (800) 227-2346
Fax (510) 523-2373

Sybex. Help Yourself.

Help Yourself with Another Quality Sybex Book

Up & Running with Windows 3.1
Joerg Schieb

A concise introduction to Windows 3.1, built on 20 steps that each take just 15 minutes to an hour to complete. Learn to install Windows 3.1, navigate the user interface, launch applications, use the File Manager, use the accessory programs, and more.

149pp; 5 7/8" x 8 1/4"
ISBN: 0-89588-843-2

Available at Better Bookstores Everywhere

Sybex Inc.
2021 Challenger Drive
Alameda, CA 94501
Telephone (800) 227-2346
Fax (510) 523-2373

Sybex. Help Yourself.

Help Yourself with Another Quality Sybex Book

Windows 3.1 Instant Reference
Marshall L. Moseley

Enjoy fast access to concise information on every Windows 3.1 mouse and keyboard command, including the accessory programs and Help facilities. Perfect for any Windows 3.1 user who needs an occasional on-the-job reminder.

262pp; 4 3/4" x 8"
ISBN: 0-89588-844-0

Available at Better Bookstores Everywhere

Sybex Inc.
2021 Challenger Drive
Alameda, CA 94501
Telephone (800) 227-2346
Fax (510) 523-2373

Sybex. Help Yourself.

Help Yourself with Another Quality Sybex Book

Understanding UNIX
For all UNIX versions, including UNIX System V Releases 3.2 & 4.0
Stan Kelly-Bootle

A user's introduction to multitasking UNIX, with a guided tour through login and basic command usage; electronic mail; customization; text editors; shells and shell programming; administration and security; and using third-party applications, such as WordPerfect and Microsoft Word. Includes complete quick-reference appendices.

638pp; 7 1/2" x 9"
ISBN: 0-89588-649-9

Available at Better Bookstores Everywhere

Sybex Inc.
2021 Challenger Drive
Alameda, CA 94501
Telephone (800) 227-2346
Fax (510) 523-2373

Sybex. Help Yourself.